JAMESTOWNE
ANCESTORS
1607 - 1699

COMMEMORATION OF THE
400th ANNIVERSARY
OF THE LANDING AT JAMES TOWNE

1607 - 2007

D1329642

Virginia Lee Hutcheson Davis

Genealogical Publishing Co., Inc.

Published by Genealogical Publishing Company
3600 Clipper Mill Rd., Suite 260
Baltimore, Maryland 21211-1953
Second, third, and fourth printings, 2006
Fifth printing, 2007
Library of Congress Catalogue Card Number 2005937849
ISBN-13: 978-0-8063-1767-0
ISBN-10: 0-8063-1767-1
Made in the United States of America

The Jamestown Church of 1639 Restored[1]

ACKNOWLEDGMENTS

This Commemoration of the 400th Anniversary of the Landing at James Towne has been the culmination of the experience gained in research of colonial tidewater Virginia by the author, Virginia Lee Hutcheson Davis[2]. Her background includes the publication of *Tidewater Virginia Families*, the compilation of the genealogy and social history of some forty early Virginia families, and *Tidewater Virginia Families: Generations Beyond*. In an effort to save early Virginia records she has been the editor and publisher of *Tidewater Virginia Families: A Magazine of History and Genealogy* (twelve volumes) and she is the compiler of the book *The Albemarle Parish Vestry Book of Surry and Sussex Counties, 1742-1786*. She is a member of the Order of Descendants of Ancient Planters, Order of First Families of Virginia, The Jamestowne Society, and The James Cittie Company. This volume is meant as an expression of appreciation of a Virginia heritage and a contribution to be shared with others who cherish their heritage and descent from these early settlers.

Over time a great deal of work has gone into the research and compilation of a listing of seventeenth-century residents of Jamestown Island. The following individuals are greatly appreciated and must be recognized for their contributions of time and expertise:

The Genealogical Publishing Company, Inc.
    Michael Tepper, Editor-in-Chief
    Eileen Perkins, Production Director
Tidewater Virginia Families Publications
    J. Thomas Wadkins III, Publishing Consultant
    James Williams Davis, Sr., for his vision
The Library of Virginia
    Lyndon Hobbs Hart, Director, Descriptive Services
    Robert Young Clay, Archivist, retired

Special recognition and appreciation are due APVA Preservation Virginia for their dedication in preserving and restoring the history and heritage that is special to Virginia. Note that much of the content of this book is available through their dedication and generosity in sharing their work for all to enjoy and learn. VLHD

PREFACE

The emergence of James Towne and Virginia began with the goals of men and their various dreams - goals as diverse as their backgrounds. These men were lesser scions of the gentry, craftsmen and laborers - all seeking a life they perceived as "better" than their present state. They may have envisioned the acquisition of land, a higher station in life, greater freedom and even gold. King James I certainly was lured by the prospect of increasing his reign with more land and wealth, and found ready participants in his dream.

After several unsuccessful earlier English colonizing efforts, King James I in 1606 issued a charter authorizing a group of investors to form the Virginia Company of London and settle colonists in North America. It was thus that his dream was fulfilled and James Towne was born. A council appointed by the king was to direct the enterprise from England, with management of day-to-day affairs in the colony entrusted to a second council of state. The charter provided that these English settlers would enjoy the same legal rights and privileges as those who remained at home.

On Saturday the twentieth of December 1606 a fleet of three ships left England. After an arduous ocean voyage, one hundred and four English colonists aboard the *Susan Constant, Godspeed* and *Discovery* reached the Virginia coast at Cape Henry. Sailing west up the river they named for their king, these men and boys stepped ashore on May 14, 1607 at the marshy peninsula now known as Jamestown Island. In time "James Towne" survived and prospered, but at first the triangular wooden palisade fort held only a tenuous foothold to the vast continent.[3]

Jamestown Island is situated in the James River, sixty-eight and three-fourths miles below the head of the tidewater, at the foot of the Richmond rapids, and fifty-eight miles above the Virginia capes. The only known map of the island and town of Jamestown (1607-1698) is the 1608 Zuniga map of Virginia (see page twelve). Present archaeological work under the auspices of The Association for the Preservation of Virginia Antiquities (APVA) *Jamestown Rediscovery*, now gives much more definitive information about the early time, character, and development of life on the island.

Much has been written earlier, as artifacts and information have unfolded, describing the land and the settlement. The archaeological work of *Jamestown Rediscovery*, directed by William M. Kelso, has provided much more definitive, exciting information than heretofore known. The maps and legends that are included in this publication help to show how this story has evolved.

The island was two and three-fourths miles long, with a width varying from approximately three hundred yards at its head to about one and one-fourth miles near its lower extremity. Originally, it held a slender connection to the mainland by a narrow neck; later this was lost to the passage of time and the erosion of the river. It is now known that the site of the fort, believed to have been lost to the ravages of the river and the elements, has survived basically intact. This provides an entirely new focus to the placement of the settlement.

The purpose of this commemorative publication is to honor those early settlers and their contributions, not only to Virginia, but also to the formation of our democratic nation and its evolution over four hundred years. Its purpose is also to include a list of all of those individuals who resided on Jamestown Island during the first almost one hundred years. Some of them lived on the Island as permanent residents very early, first in tents, then in post-in-ground houses, and later in more elegant brick houses. Others lived on the Island only part time, due to their function in the governmental affairs of the colony.

The seat of government for the colony was first located in James Towne, then later moved to Williamsburg. The several locations of the state house are now known, and the site of many of the houses of the members of the General Assembly have been identified. From the foundation that remained of the earliest Jamestown church a memorial replica church has been erected and is now the focal point of the island community.

A list of all the individuals who can be documented as having lived on the Island between 1607 and 1699, either as land owners or as members of the House of Burgesses or as other officials is presented here. The information presented here is not intended to be all-inclusive; it includes only those who can be documented as having lived in that time and on Jamestown Island. This list can be used as a starting point for those interested in establishing eligibility for membership in a number of hereditary societies that require descent from an individual's early Virginia ancestor.

One should realize that the information in this list only serves as documentation, as found available, of that person's presence and service. It has been confirmed in so far as is possible with available extant records; however, the list by its very nature, cannot be an all inclusive list of the early ancestors. The dates recorded cannot be construed as precise, nor should there be restrictions placed by the dates presented here. Where inclusive dates are shown, the individual may not have served continuously in that position. The Julian calendar for dating is used throughout the early history.

These ancestors' names may be verified and documented as to residence and service from a variety of accepted sources. A list of acceptable references is included for those interested in verification and documentation of service. The word "service" refers to a position held by the ancestor as Governor, Secretary of State, a member of the General Assembly, Burgess, Council, clergyman, or other position of significance to the colonial government.

In this list the names of early settlers are arranged alphabetically. Where there are variations in the spelling, the most common and readily identifiable variant has been used . Keep in mind that during the early colonial period names were spelled phonetically and different variants were used within the same document. Also it must be noted that not everyone in this list had descendants.

The *fl* symbol is not used here, in deference to the possibility of more definitive dates of service. The following symbols have been used: b. born, d. died, l. living, c. circa, when approximate date is known, bef. before, aft. after. The use of the designation "place" refers to the place of residence of not only those who lived on Jamestown Island, but also those who served in some official capacity and resided elsewhere, i.e., the county, hundred or plantation.

The 1608 map of James Fort (page twelve) and the diagram of the site (page thirteen) show the original settlement and the progression of present-day archaeological work undertaken there. The research continues, and new information has resulted in a greater understanding of the site of James Towne on Jamestown Island and the development of the colony. The other maps included here show the geographic growth of the colony beyond Jamestown Island throughout the seventeenth century, first as shires then as plantations and hundreds. From this, one can determine the areas where the early ancestors selected the land for their home sites and plantations. Further geographic division into counties became necessary during the century as the population grew.

It is hoped that this book of Commemoration for the 400th anniversary of the settlement of James Towne will honor our early ancestors and inspire all of us to be worthy of the heritage of Jamestown in Virginia, the genesis of our United States of America.

Virginia Lee Hutcheson Davis

ANCIENT PLANTERS[4]

The following list is made up of those who are known to have come to Virginia before the close of the year 1616, survived the massacre, appear in the Muster of 1624/1625 as then living in Virginia, and to whom the designation "Ancient Planter" may with justification be applied (see Descriptive Terms). Those so identified in the work of Nell Marion Nugent, *Cavaliers and Pioneers* include the date, or documented designation of Ancient Planter, with year not determined (ynd), or by special consideration (gov). They have been alphabetized for ease of search for specific ancestors. Others listed are those included in the research of the Order of Descendants of Ancient Planters (odap). It is believed that all of these set foot on land at Jamestown and lived there, though briefly, until they could safely venture to outlying areas and claim land after 1616. In listing the names they will be identified as to the source of their eligibility for inclusion in this list.[5]

Giles Allington ynd	John Brewer odap
William Andrews ynd	Richard Brewster odap
William Askew 1610	Richard Buck, Rev. odap
Henry Bagwell 1608	William Burditt odap
Thomas Bagwell ynd	John Burrows odap
William Baker 1609	William Capps ynd
John Bainham 1616	Nathaniel Cawsey 1608
Michael Batt(s) odap	Thomasine Cawsey 1609
William Bayley 1610	Isaac Chaplaine 1611
Thomas Baywell ynd	Francis Chapman 1608
Mary Beheathland odap	William Claiborne gov
Robert Beheathland odap	John Chandler 1609
Theophilis Beriston 1614	Edward Clark ynd
Richard Biggs 1610	Phettiplace Clause 1608
Richard Birchett 1615	John Clay 1613
Reynold Booth 1609	Joseph Cobb odap
Mary Boulding odap	Francis Cole 1616
Thomas Boulding odap	Susan Collins 1613
William Boulding 1610	Henry Coltman 1610
Richard Boulton 1610	William Coxe 1610
Cheyney Boyce ynd	Raleigh Croshaw 1608

ANCIENT PLANTERS
James Davis, Capt. ynd
Rachel Davis odap
Henry Dawkes 1608
Adam Dixon 1612
John Dodds 1607
John Downman 1611
Thomas Dowse odap
Elizabeth Dunthorne 1610
Clement Evand 1616
Margery Fairfax 1611
William Fairfax 1611
Thomas Farmer 1616
Cecily Jordan Farrar 1610
Robert Fisher 1611
Mary Flint ynd
Pharoah Flinton 1612
John Flood 1610
William Gany odap
Thomas Garnett 1610
Thomas Gates, Sir 1609
Thomas Godby 1608
Thomas Graves 1608
Thomas Gray 1608
Robert Greenleaf 1610
Edward Grendon ynd
John Grundy 1611
Mary Grundy 1616
Edward Gurgany odap
Adria Gurgany odap
Thomas Harris ynd
John Hatton 1613
Walter Heyley odap
Nicholas Hospkins 1616
Bartholomew Hospkins
Oliver Jenkins 1611
John Johnson ynd
Elizabeth Jones 1609
Samuel Jordan 1610

continued
William Julian 1608
Martha Key ynd
Thomas Key 1619 (sic)
Richard Kingsmill odap
Thomas Lane 1613
William Lansden ynd
Ann Burrus Laydon 1608
John Laydon 1607
John Lightfoot 1610
Albiano Lupo 1610
Elizabeth Lupo 1616
Francis Mason 1613
Cornelius Maye 1616
William Morgan 1611
Alexander Mountney 1610
Susan Old 1616
Isabella Smyth Pace odap
Richard Pace odap
William Parker 1616
Robert Partin 1609
Francis Paul ynd
William Perry 1611
William Pierce 1616
John Poole, Jr. odap
Robert Poole, Sr. odap
John Powell odap
John Price odap
Miles Pricket 1611
John Proctor 1610
John Rolfe odap
Christopher Safford 1613
Joanne Salford 1611
John Salford 1616
Robert Salford 1611
Sarah Salford 1616
Thomas Savage 1608
Samuel Sharpe 1610
William Sharpe odap

John Sleight 1610
John Smith 1607
John Smith 1611
John Smith gov
Roger Smith odap
William Sparkes 1616
William Spencer odap
Thomas Spelman 1616
Thomas Stepney 1610
Thomas Sully 1611
John Taylor 1608
Richard Taylor 1608
Thomas Thornbury 1616
Henry Tucker 1615
William Tucker 1610

Henry Turner odap
Thomas Turner 1616
Amyle Waine 1610
John Ward ynd
Edward Waters 1608
William Waters odap
Francis West 1610
Temperance Flowerdew
    Yeardley West ynd
Henry Williams 1613
Thomas Wiloughby 1610
John Woodlief odap
Robert Wright 1608
George Yeardley, Sir 1609
Richard Yonge 1616

HEREDITARY SOCIETIES QUALIFYING[6]
FOR DESCENT FROM JAMESTOWN, 1607-1699

Order of Descendants of Ancient Planters
Order of First Families of Virginia
National Society Colonial Dames XVII Century
National Society of Colonial Daughters of the Seventeenth Century
The Colonial Dames of America
The Jamestowne Society
The National Society of the Colonial Dames of America
Order of the Founders and Patriots of America
National Society Daughters of Founders and Patriots of America
National Society of Sons of the American Colonists
Society of the Descendants of the Colonial Clergy
Vermont Society of Colonial Dames
Order of Americans of Armorial Ancestry
National Society of the Dames of the Court of Honor
General Society of Colonial Wars
National Society Daughters of Colonial Wars

NOVA BRITANNIA.

OFFERING MOST

Excellent fruites by Planting in
VIRGINIA.

Exciting all such as be well affected
to further the same.

LONDON
Printed for SAMVEL MACHAM, and are to be sold at
his Shop in Pauls Church-yard, at the
Signe of the Bul-head.
1609.

1609 Advertisement[7]

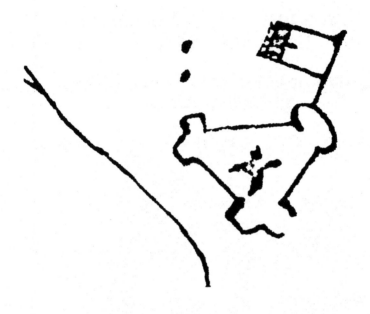

Zuniga's Map of James Fort 1608[8]

      This rendering appears on a tracing of a 1608 John Smith map of Virginia. It is the earliest known map of Virginia, and was sent to Philip III of Spain by his ambassador, Pedro de Zuniga. Previously, historians and archaeologists took this tiny drawing as a representative icon only; a simple sketch of a fort with a very out-of-scale flag. But a closer look presented the strong possibility that the triangular defense had two watch towers on the river, the "x" or cross marked the church, and the "flag," with the field at the wrong end, was actually a plan of an enclosed settlement or garden to the north.

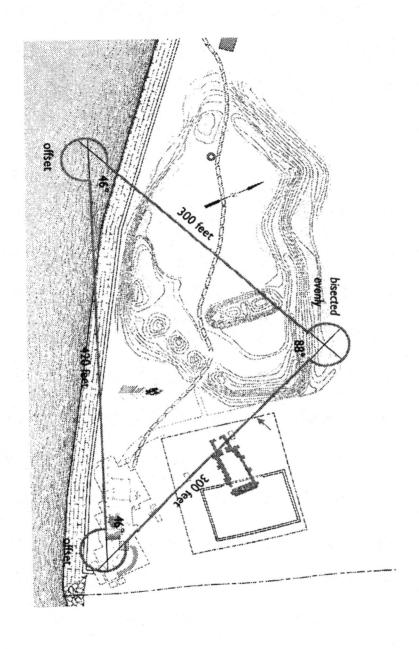

James Fort[9]
Plotted from the Jamestown Rediscovery Archaeological Studies, 2003

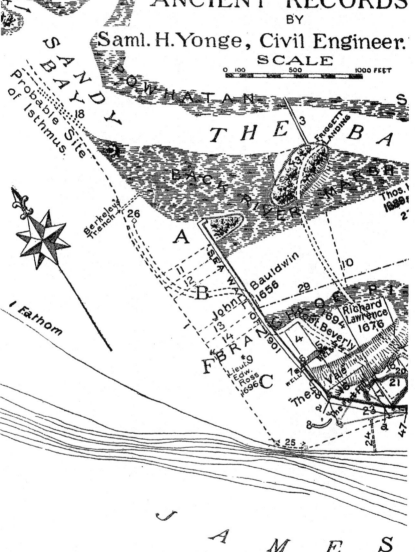

Map of James Citty, Virginia[10]

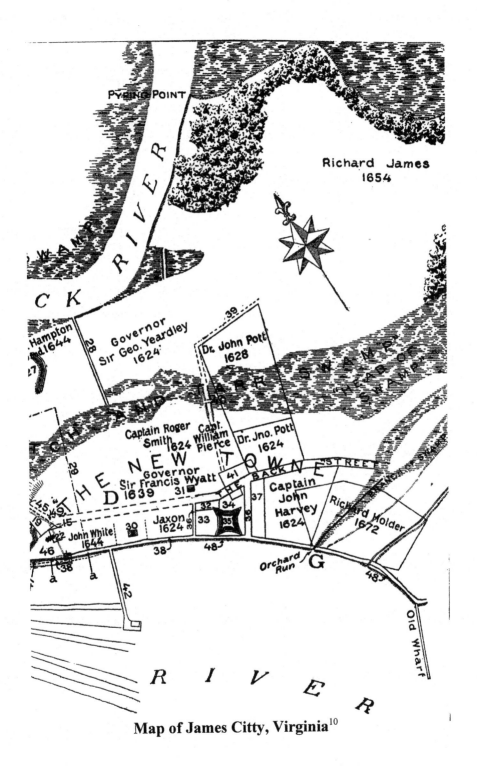

Map of James Citty, Virginia[10]

KEY TO MAP OF JAMES CITTY, VA., 1607 - 1698[11]

A - First ridge, "Block House Hill," belonging to John Bauldwin in 1656.
B - Second ridge, containing tracts of Richard James, John Bauldwin,
Rev. Thomas Hampton, *et al.*
C - Third ridge, on which stood the third and fourth state houses.
D - Fourth ridge, on which the town was principally situated.
E - (not found on map, identified in the text only as a narrow slash , ed.)*
F - (identified only in the text as a ridge with an easterly trend narrow slash, ed.)*
G - (identified only in the text as a branch of a great marsh, ed.)*
a,a,a,a, - Jetties constructed in 1895-96 to protect island bank.
1- Approximated position of western shore line of island, 1600-1700.
2 - Present shore line of mainland above the island.
3 - Bridge across Back River on road to Williamsburg.
4 - Lot of Philip Ludwell, Esq., in 1694, containing the ruins of three brick houses.
5 - Third and fourth state houses, 1666 to 1698.
6 - "Country House," in 1694.
7 - Part of foundations of building reputed to have been a powder magazine.
8 - Site of brick fort constructed between 1670 and 1676.
9 - The lone cypress.
10 - Approximate position of northerly line between Richard James and John
Bauldwin in 1657.
11 - Approximate site of tract of Richard Saunders, 1644.
12 - Approximate site of tract of Edward Challis, 1643.
13 - Approximate site of tract of Radulph Spraggon, 1644.
14 - Approximate site of tract of Geo. Gilbert, 1643.
15 - Probable outline of original paled four-acre town, shown by red (sic) lines.
16 - Tract of Edward Chilton, Attorney-General, 1683.
17 - Tract of Wm. Edwards, Sr., 1690.
18 - Piles of former bridge between island and mainland, constructed during first
half of nineteenth century.
19 - Tract of John Howard, 1694.
20 - Tract of Nathaniel Bacon, Sr., 1694. Contains foundatin of chimney.
21 - Confederate fort constructed in 1861.
22 - Ancient tower ruin, inclosed part of old graveyard, and foundation of third,
fourth and fifth church.
23 - Probable site of triangluar fort constructed in 1607, designated in 18th century
MS, "Fort Hill".
24 - Probably site of "bridge" (wharf), constructed by Dale in 1611.
25 - Probably landing place of first settlers, May 14, 1607, indicated by red flags
(Not shown).
26 - Approximate site of blockhouse, built by Captain Richard Stephens in 1624,
and probable site of Berkeley's trench.
27 - Confederate redoubt commanding Back River, constructed in 1861.
28 - Modern ditch draining "Pitch and Tarr Swamp".
29 - Boundary lines of tract belonging to the Association for the Preservation of
Virginia Antiquities.

30 - "The old state house" (approximate), used from about 1630 to 1656, on one-acre tract, of which part was sold to Ludwell and Stegg in 1667. Most probably contained Gov. Harvey's residence prior to 1641, Gov. Berkeley's residence prior to 1656 and subsequently Gov. Bennett's residence.

31 - Ruins of building on site of Ambler-Jacquelin messuage.

32 - Tract of John Chew, 1624.

33 - Tract of Captain Richard Stephens, 1623.

34 - Tract of Captain Ralph Hamor, 1624, Secretary of State and chronicler.

35 - Site of turf fort, erected probably about 1663.

36 - Cross streets connecting "the way along the Maine River" and the Back Street.

37 - Tract of George Menefy, 1624, member of the Council of State.

38 - The "way along the Greate river," or "Maine river."

39 - Cart track "leading to Island House," in 1665.

40 - Causeway over swamp formerly connecting part of island containing "the new towne" with the second ridge.

41 - One-acre tract bought by William Sherwood in 1681, "on which formerly stood the brick house formerly called the Country House," and later, probably Sherwood's residence.

42 - Jamestown Island wharf.

43 - Probable site of tract of Richard Clarke, 1646.

44 - The "main cart path."

45 - "The old Greate Road," in 1694.

46 - Ancient graveyard.

47 - Point where skeltons were exposed by bank abrasion in 1895.

48 - Shore line of 1903.

49 - Traces of house foundations. Probable site of Richard Lawrence's dwelling about 1676.

N.B. Broken lines on map indicate approximate boundaries, etc.

* The descriptions of the locations of E, F and G that appear on the map may be found on pages 22 and 23 in the text of the book *The Site of Old "James Towne"*.

Note: All dates are given according to Old Style. The quotations are as presented in the original descriptions of the places. Articles entitled *The Site of Old 'James Towne,' 1607 - 1698,"* originally appeared in four consecutive issues of the Virginia Magazine of History and Biography, between January and October, 1904.

Samuel H. Yonge, the author of the book of that title was one of the best known engineers of his day and planned and superintended the construction of the sea wall protecting the upper end of Jamestown Island, thus saving from the relentless river the old Church tower. He also located and excavated the first foundations uncovered on the historic site.

Mr. Yonge writes: *The credit of rescuing from oblivion and preserving some of the most important ancient landmarks of Virginia is entirely due to the Association for the Preservation of Virginia Antiquities.*

SETTLEMENTS IN VIRGINIA BEFORE 1624[12]
Early place names before shire formation

x Jamestowne* Island
Jamestown

Elizabeth City
Accawmack
(Eastern Shore)
Nansemond
Kecoughtan
Newport News
Blunt Point

James City
Mulberry Island
Martin's Hundred
Archer's Hope
Neck of Land
Argall Town
Pasbehegh
The Main
Pace's Paines
Burrow's Mount
Treasurer's Plantation
Crowder's Plantation
Blaney's Plantation
Roger Smith's Plantation
Mathew's Plantation
Hog Island
Lawne's Plantation
Warrascoyack
Basse's Choice

Charles City
Smith's Hundred
Weyanoke
Swinhows
Westover
Berkeley Hundred
Causey's Care
Shirley Hundred
Upper Hundred or Curls
Digg's Hundred
Piercey's Hundred
Jourdan's Journey
Woodleefe's Plantation
Chaplain's Choice
Truelove's Plantation
Merchant's Hope
Maycock's Plantation
Flowerdieu Hundred
Capt. Spillman's Divident
Ward's Plantation
Martin's Brandon

Henrico
Henrico
Arrahatock
College Lands
The Falls
Falling Creek
Sheffield's Plantation
Proctor's Plantation
Coxendale
Bermuda Hundred

*Note: the spelling of places
varied with usage

18

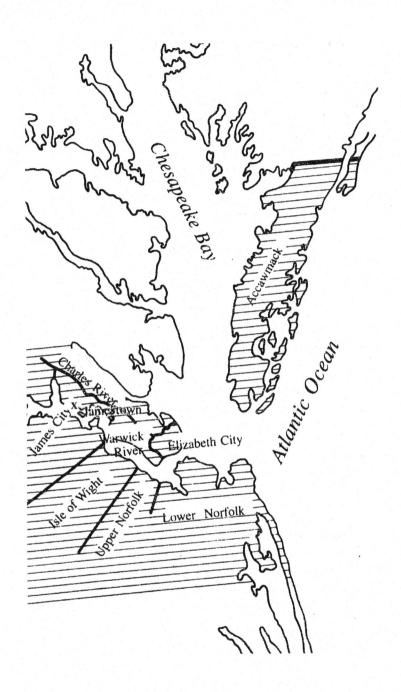

Map of the James River Counties in Virginia 1634[13]

19

1. Accawmack (*original shire*)
   A. Became Northampton in 1642/43
   B. Accomack 1661
2. Charles City (*original shire*)
   A. Charles City County
3. Charles River (*original shire*)
   A. became York 1642/3
   B. Northumberland 1645
      1. Northumberland after 1655
      2. Lancaster 1651
         a. Lancaster after 1673
         b. Middlesex 1673
      3. Rappahannock (Old) 1657 name abolished 1692
         a. Essex 1692
         b. Richmond 1692
      4. Westmoreland 1653
         a. Westmoreland after 1664
         b. Stafford 1664
   C. Gloucester 1652
      1. Gloucester after 1691
      2. King and Queen 1691
   D. New Kent 1654 (part of James City)
      1. New Kent
4. Elizabeth City (*original shire*)
   A. Elizabeth City
   B. Lower Norfolk 1637
      1. Norfolk after 1691
      2. Princess Anne 1691
   C. Upper Norfolk 1637
      Later called Nansemond 1642
5. Henrico (*original shire*)
6. James City County (*original shire*)
   A. James City after 1652
   B. Surry 1652
7. Warrascoyack (*original shire*)
   Later called Isle of Wight 1637
8. Warwick River (*original shire*)
   Later called Warwick 1642/3

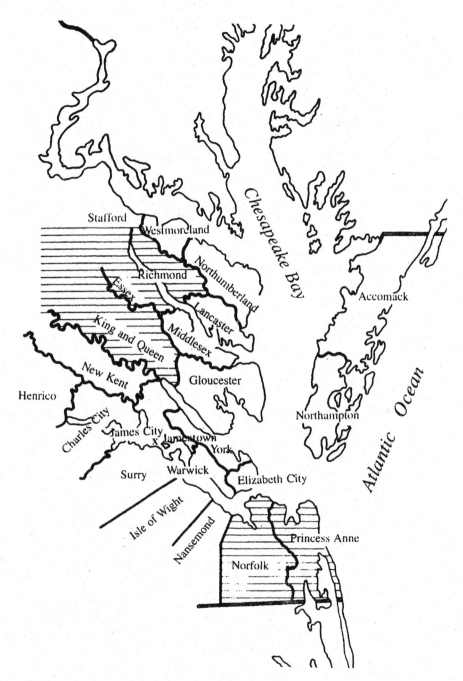

Virginia Original Counties, 1634 With Divisions Until 1700[15]

21

EXPLANATION OF DESCRIPTIVE TERMS

Ancient Planter. A colonist in Virginia before 1616, entitled to 100 acres of land provided he paid his own passage and had dwelt in the colony for three years when application for land was made. In accordance with a predetermined policy of the Virginia Company, no individual assignments of land were made during the first seven years of the colony's existence. The policy of granting patents for acreage to settlers was inaugurated during the latter part of the regime of Sir Thomas Dale, Governor, 1611-1616.

Calendar. The Julian calendar, according to which 25 March was reckoned as the first day of the New Year, was in use together with the Gregorian calendar until 1752 when it was abandoned and the 11 days difference between the two calendars was dropped out of the year. The occurrence of an event between 1 January, the first day of the New Year according to the Gregorian calendar and 25 March, the New Year's day of the Julian calendar, is indicated by a diagonal, thus: 16 February 1624/25, which shows that the event took place on 16 February 1624 by the Julian, but 1625 by the Gregorian calendar.

Council. An advisory group of leading men dwelling in Virginia, appointed by the king, to assist the governor in the direction of the Company's business affecting the Colony of Virginia.

Council of Virginia. Thirteen members of the Virginia Company originally appointed by King James, as specified in the First Charter (1606), to handle from England the direction of the Company's business affecting the Colony of Virginia.

Counties. In 1623-33, twenty-one plantations or hundreds were represented in the Assembly, and in 1634 these and others were grouped in units and the colony divided into eight shires or counties to be governed as the shires in England. They were: Accawmack, Charles City, Charles River, Elizabeth City, Henrico, James City, Warrosquyoake, and Warwick River. As the population grew and began to spread, areas were cut off from these original eight shires and additional counties were formed, and the names began to appear more as they are known today. See the progression of counties shown here.

Hundreds. A term used in a more liberal sense than in England where it referred to a county district authorized to hold court. The large early plantations, patents for which were issued in the names of several persons often were designated "hundreds," such as Martin's Hundred in James City, Smith's (Southampton) Hundred on the north side of the Chickahominy River, Flowerdieu Hundred, Governor Yeardley's Plantation, Berkeley Hundred on the James River and Bermuda

22

Hundred at the mouth of the Appomattox River.

Muster. After the Indian massacre of March 1621/22 a letter was sent to London informing the authorities of the killing of 347 persons in the uprising. In order that the heirs might have speedy access to their inheritance of estates and lands, a listing was ordered of those persons slain and of those who remained alive. Thus the Muster of the Inhabitants of Virginia was taken between 20 January and 7 February 1624/5. When Captain John Harvey, who had directed the listing, left Virginia by 16 February 1624/25 he carried with him reports from the 21 plantations, which gave a good approximation of the condition of the colony at that time. Hence the Muster is a document pertinent both to the Virginia Company's administration in Virginia and to the termination of the authority of this corporation, composed mostly of London merchants who, in 1606, had been given a royal charter to establish a colony in the New World.

Spelling. There was no standardized spelling in the seventeenth century. The same word may vary in spelling on the same page. Proper names especially were subject to variations. Adherence to seventeenth-century spelling in documents will account for the variations of spelling of names in this register.

Virginia Company of London Dissolution.[16] From the beginning King James I had favored the colonial enterprise, but as the colony grew in importance and at the same time began to assume the rudiments of self-government, he and his immediate advisers began to view with alarm the growing independence of the colony under the guidance of the Earl of Southampton. A Court party headed by the Earl of Warwick supporting the king's views developed within the Company and strong influence was brought to bear for surrender of the Company's Charter. The Indian massacre and ensuing troubles in Virginia gave weight to the king's position.[17] On 17 November 1623 the Royal Commissioners for Virginia ordered the surrender of the locked trunk containing the Company's records. When the Company refused to surrender its Charter for Virginia, the case was placed in the hands of Attorney-General Coventry, who prepared a *quo warranto* against the Company. The Court hearing the case decreed that "the Patent or Charter of the Company of English merchants trading to Virginia ...there, should thenceforth be null and void." However, this judgment was not entered on the record until 1632 when it was done at the insistance of Lord Baltimore; in 1640 the patent for Maryland was taken out under the Virginia patent under the Broad Seal of England. It continued as a basis for rights to land and laws.

Notes:

1. George Carrington Mason, *Colonial Churches of Tidewater Virginia.* 1945 (Richmond, VA: Whittet and Shepperson) frontispiece.

2. Virginia Lee Hutcheson Davis, *Tidewater Virginia Families; Tidewater Virginia Families: Generations Beyond.* 1989, 1998, 4th printing 2004 (Baltimore: Genealogical Publishing Company). *Albemarle Parish Vestry Book, Surry and Sussex Counties, 1742-1786.* 2005 (Baltimore: Clearfield Company). Editor/Publisher, *Tidewater Virginia Families: A Magazine of History and Genealogy.* Volumes 1-12, 1992-2004.

3. Hume, Ivor Noel, *The Virginia Adventure.* 1994 (New York: Alfred A. Knopf) 121-126.

4. Nell Marion Nugent, *Cavaliers and Pioneers, Abstracts of Virginia Land Patents and Grants Volume 1.* 1934 (Richmond, VA: Press of The Dietz Printing Co.) xxvi-xxxiv.

5. Elizabeth Tissot, Registrar, Order of Descendants of Ancient Planters. *Directory of the National Society Order of Descendants of Ancient Planters.* 2004-2006 np.

6. Robert R. Davenport, Editor, *Hereditary Society Blue Book.* 1994 (Baltimore: Genealogical Publishing Company).

7. Lewis Paul Todd and Merle Curti, *Rise of the American Nation.* 1950 (New York: Harcourt, Brace and World, Inc.) 27.

8. William M. Kelso, *Jamestown Rediscovery I.* 1995 (Richmond, VA: Association for the Preservation of Virginia Antiquities) 10.

9. William M. Kelso and Beverly Straube, *Jamestown Rediscovery 8.* 2004 (Richmond, VA: The Association for the Preservation of Virginia Antiquities) 36, 80. As plotted from the Jamestown Rediscovery Archaeological Studies 1995-2005.

10. Samuel H. Yonge, *The Site of Old "James Towne" 1607-1698.* 1901, 1907, 1930 (Richmond, VA: The Association for the Preservation of Virginia Antiquities) foldout map. Commemorative Edition, 1907, Jamestown, 300th Anniversary.

11. Yonge ibid. 18,19.

12. Charles E. Hatch, Jr., *The First Seventeen Years Virginia, 1607-1624.* 1957 (Charlottesville, VA: The University Press of Virginia) 32-33.

13. Michael F. Doran, *Atlas of County Boundary Changes in Virginia, 1634-1895.* 1987 (Athens, GA: Iberian Publishing Co, now New Papyrus Publishing Co.) by permission from John Vogt, CEO New Papyrus Co. 6-7. Source: M.P. Robinson, *Virginia Counties: Those Resulting from Virginia Legislation. Bulletin of the Virginia State Library.* 1916, Volume 9, 1,2,3. 93-94.

14. Doran, Vogt ibid. 14-15.

15. John H. Gwathmey, *Twelve Virginia Counties.* 1937, rep. 1997 (Baltimore: Genealogical Publishing Co.) 7, 37, 85, 123, 149.

16. Anticipating this move on the part of the king, Nicholas Farrar some six months earlier procured an expert clerk to copy all of the company's records. The surviving records, later transcribed and published by Susan Myra Kingsbury in four volumes, may be found at the Library of Congress.

17. Virginia M. Meyer and John Frederick Dorman, *Adventurers of Purse and Person.* Third Edition. 1987 (Richmond, VA: Order of First Families of Virginia) xxiii-xxvii. First Edition. 1956. Compiled and edited by Annie Lash Jester in collaboration with Martha Woodroof Hiden.

RECOMMENDED FOR RESEARCH
FOR DOCUMENTATION ON SERVICE,
DATE AND COUNTY/PLACE

Alexander Brown. *The Genesis of the United States.* 2 vols. Boston: Houghton, Mifflin & Co., 1891.

William Walter Hening. *Statutes at Large.* Volumes I-V. Richmond, VA: Whittet & Shepperson, 1896.

Cynthia Leonard. *The General Assembly of Virginia - a Bicentennial Register of Members.* Richmond, VA: Published for the General Assembly of Virginia by the Virginia State Library, 1978.

H.R. McIlwaine, editor. *Journals of The House of Burgesses, 1619 to 1658/59*; 1659-1693; 1695-1702. Richmond, VA: The Colonial Press, 1913-1915.

H.R. McIlwaine, editor. *Minutes of the Council and General Court of Colonial Virginia, 1622-1632; 1670-1676; 1683.* Richmond, VA: Virginia State Library. 1st ed., 1924; 2nd ed., 1979.

Virginia M. Meyer & John Frederick Dorman. *Adventurers of Purse and Person.* 3rd ed. Richmond, VA: Order of First Families of Virginia, 1987; 4th ed. John Frederick Dorman, editor. Baltimore: Genealogical Publishing Co., Inc. Vol. 1 2004; Vol. 2, 2005.

Nell Marion Nugent. *Cavaliers and Pioneers, Abstracts of Land Patents and Grants.* Vol.1: 1623-1666. Baltimore: Genealogical Publishing Co., Inc., 1963, repr. Vol. 2: 1666-1695. Richmond, VA: Virginia State Library, 1977.

William G. and Mary N. Stanard. *Colonial Virginia Register.* Albany, NY: J. Munsell's Sons, 1902.

JAMESTOWNE ANCESTORS

A

Ancestor Name	Time Period and Role	Origin or County Represented
Abbot, Samuel		
	1643-1647, 1648 Clerk of Council	Jamestowne Island
Abrahall, Richard		
	1654-1662 Burgess	New Kent
Abrell, Robert		
	1654-1655 Burgess	New Kent
Adams, Thomas		
	b.1586, d.1668 Draper's Company Letter, Stockholder	Shropshire, England
Addams, Robert		
	1624 Burgess	Martin's Hundred
Allen, Arthur		
	1682-1688 Burgess, Speaker of House of Burgesses	Surry
Allen, William		
	1629 Burgess	Henry Throgmorton's Plantation
Allerton, Willoughby		
	1699 Burgess	Westmoreland
Allerton/Alerton, Isaac		
	1683, 1696-1697, d.1702 Councillor, Burgess	Westmoreland
Allomby, Thomas		
	1684-1691 Burgess	Elizabeth City
Alsop, James		
	1689 Landowner	Jamestowne Island

27

Anderson, John
  1685-1686   no place listed (n.p.l.)
  Burgess
Anderson, William
  1685-1686   Accomack
  Burgess
Andrews, Joakin
  1620, 1643   Jamestowne Island
  Landowner
Andrews, William
  bef.1616, 1663-1664   Northampton
  Ancient Planter, Burgess
Andros, Edmund, Sir
  1637-d.c.1692   Jamestowne Island
  Governor
Appleton, John
  1674-1676   Westmoreland
  Burgess
Applewhaite, Henry
  b.1643-d.1702   Isle of Wight
  Burgess
Archer, Gabriel
  1607-1609   Jamestowne Island
  Councillor, Recorder
Argall, Samuel, Sir.
  1572-1617   Jamestowne Island
  Councillor, Governor
Armistead, Anthony
  1682,1693-1699   Elizabeth City
  Burgess
Armistead, John
  1680, 1685-86   Gloucester
  Burgess
Armistead, William, Jr.
  1692-1693   Elizabeth City
  Burgess
Arunell, John
  1633   Elizabeth City
  Burgess

Ashton, Peter

| | 1656, 1660 | Elizabeth City |
| | Burgess | Northumberland |

Aston, Walter

| | 1607-1656 | Charles City |
| | Burgess | |

Atkins, John

| | 1630 | Warroscoyack |
| | Burgess | |

Awborne, Richard

| | 1668-1671 | n.p.l. |
| | Clerk | |

Awbrey, Henry

| | 1682-1692 | Rappahannock |
| | Burgess | |

B

Bacon, Nathaniel, Sr.

| | 1619-1687 | York |
| | Burgess | |

Bacon, Nathaniel, Jr.

	1657, 1675, 1676	Henrico, York
	Councillor, Burgess	
	President of Council	

Bagnall, James

| | 1646, 1654-1655 | Isle of Wight |
| | Burgess | Lancaster |

Bagwell, Henry

| | 1589-1663 | Northampton |
| | Ancient Planter | |

Bagwell, Thomas

| | bef.1616, 1629, 1630 | Pasbehegh |
| | Ancient Planter, Burgess | Accomack |

Baker, Henry

| | 1693 | Isle of Wight |
| | Burgess | |

Baker, Lawrence
1661-1676		Surry
Burgess		

Baldridge, Thomas
1651-1652		Northumberland
Burgess		

Baldry, Robert
1660, 1661-1676		York
Burgess		

Baldwin, John
1637		Jamestowne Island
Landowner		

Baley, Temperance
c.1617-1652		Henrico
Muster of 1624/5		

Ball, Henry
1646		Elizabeth City
Burgess		

Ball, Joseph
1693, 1698		Lancaster
Burgess		

Ball, William
1615-1680		Lancaster
Burgess		

Ballard, Thomas
1630-1670-1689		James City, York
Burgess, Member of Council		

Balthropp, Christopher
1644		York
Burgess		

Barbar, William
1661-1676, d.1677		York
Burgess		

Barber, Francis
1688		York
Burgess		

Barber, John
1657, 1667		Jamestowne Island
Landowner		

Barber, Thomas

    1680-1696   York
    Burgess

Barham, Anthony

    1630   Mulberry Island
    Burgess

Barker, William

    1645-1646   Charles City
    Burgess

Barkham, Edward, Sir

    d.by 1634   Norfolk, England
    Stockholder Virginia Company

Barnard, Thomas

    1640   Warwick River
    Burgess

Barne, William, Sir

    1568-1619   County Kent, England
    Stockholder Virginia Company

Barnes, Lancelott

    1630   Lower Elizabeth City
    Burgess

Barnett, Thomas

    1632,1642   Stanley Hundred
    Burgess   Warwick River

Barrett, William

    1645, 1646, 1649   James City
    Burgess

Barrington, Robert

    1628, 1630   James City
    Burgess

Bartley, Edward

    1625   Hogg Island
    Burgess

Bassett, William

    1693, 1696-1699   New Kent
    Burgess

Bates, John

    bef.1616, 1623-1667   York
    Ancient Planter, Muster of 1624/5

Batt(e), Henry

	1685-1692, 1695 Burgess	Charles City

Batt, Michael

	bef.1616, 1643 Ancient Planter, Landowner	Jamestowne Island

Batt, William

	1654-1655 Burgess	Surry

Battaile, John

	1693, 1696-1697 Burgess	Essex

Batte, Henry

	1685-1686 Burgess	Prince George

Batte, William

	1659 Burgess	Elizabeth City

Baugh, John

	1642, 1645 Burgess	Henrico

Baughan, James

	1698-1712 Burgess	Essex

Bayley, Richard

	1693, 1696-1699 Burgess	Accomack

Baylor, John

	1693 Burgess	Gloucester

Bayly, Arthur

	1638, 1643 Landowner, Burgess	Jamestowne Island Henrico

Bayly, John

	d.by 1623/24 Resident of Jamestowne	James City

Bayly, Mary

	c.1619-1643 Resident prior to Muster	James City

Baynham, Alexander

    1654-1655   Westmoreland
    Burgess

Beale, Thomas

    1662, d.after 1676   York
    Councillor

Beazley, Job

    1656   Isle of Wight
    Burgess

Beheathland, Robert

    d.by 1627   Jamestowne Island
    Original Jamestowne Settler

Benn, James

    1692, 1696-99   Warrascoyack
    Burgess

Bennett, Alice ——— Pierce

    c.1621-1647   Isle of Wight
    Living in Virginia bef. Muster

Bennett, Edward

    b.1577-d.by 1663   Somerset, England
    Stockholder, Auditor, Virginia Company
    1628 Burgess   Warrascoyack

Bennett, Philip

    1645-1646   Upper Norfolk
    Burgess

Bennett, Richard

    1608-1675   Nansemond
    Burgess, Governor, Councillor

Bennett, Samuel

    b.1585-d.by 1636   Elizabeth City
    Living at Muster of 1624/5

Bennett, Thomas

    1632   Mulberry Island
    Burgess

Bentley, William

    bef.1616, 1629   Nutmegg Quarter
    Ancient Planter, Burgess

Berkeley, John

    1621   Jamestowne Island
    Councillor

Berkeley, William, Sir
| | 1606-1662 | James City |
| | Governor | |

Bernard, Thomas
| | 1644-1646 | Warwick |
| | Burgess | |

Bernard, William
	1641-1665	Basse's Choice
	Muster of 1624/5	
	Councillor	Isle of Wight

Beverley, Robert
| | 1641-1686 | Middlesex |
| | Councillor | |

Beverly, Peter
| | 1691-1697 | Middlesex |
| | Clerk | |

Bickley, Francis, Sir
	b.1582/3	Cambridgeshire, England
	d.1670	Norfolk, England
	Stockholder in Virginia Company	

Biggs, Richard
| | bef.1616, 1624-1625 | Shirley Hundred |
| | Ancient Planter, Burgess | |

Bishop, John
| | 1644,1652-1653,d.by 1656 | Charles City |
| | Burgess | |

Biss, James
| | 1680-1682 | Charles City |
| | Burgess | |

Blackey, William
| | 1658-1676 | New Kent |
| | Burgess | |

Blair, James
| | 1689 | James City |
| | Councillor | |

Blake, John
| | 1666-1676 | Nansemond |
| | Burgess | |

Bland, John

        1572-1632   London, England
        Member Virginia Company

Bland, Peregrine

        1640   Charles River
        Burgess

Bland, Richard

        1693   Charles City
        Burgess

Bland, Theodrick

        1630-1671   Charles City
        Burgess, Councillor

Blaney, Edward

        1624-1625   Plantations Over Water
        1626, 1627   Jamestowne Island
        Councillor, Burgess

Blaney, Mary

        1620, 1628   Jamestowne Island
        Landowner

Blewitt, ———

        1620   Jamestowne Island
        Councillor

Bohun, Lawrence, Dr.

        1620   Jamestowne Island
        Councillor

Boise/Boyce, Cheney

        bef.1616, 1629-1631   Shirley Hundred
        Ancient Planter, Burgess

Boisseau, James, the Rev.

        b.c.1660, 1.1692   France
        Vestryman   Prince George

Bolling, Robert

        1646-1709   Prince George
        1688-1692, 1699   Charles City
        Burgess

Bond, John

        1654-1662   Isle of Wight
        Burgess

Booth, Robert, Dr.

   1616-1657   York
   Burgess

Borne, Robert

   1658   York
   Burgess

Boucher, Daniel

   1653 d.1668   Isle of Wight
   Burgess

Bowler, Thomas

   d.1679   Rappahannock
   Councillor

Boyse, John

   1619   Martin's Hundred
   Burgess

Boyse, Luke

   1624-1625 Neck of Land, James City
   Burgess

Bracewell/Braswell, Robert

   1653, d.1668   Isle of Wight
   Burgess, Minister

Bradwell, John

   1637   Jamestowne Island
   Landowner

Branch, Christopher

   b.1602-d.1672   Henrico
   Muster of 1624/5, Burgess

Branch, John

   1642-1643   Elizabeth City
   Burgess

Brassier, James

   1684   Nansemond
   Burgess

Brassieur, John

   1680-1697   Nansemond
   Burgess

Bray, James

   1670, 1688, 1691   James City
   Burgess, Councillor

Bray, Robert

  1676   Lower Norfolk
  Burgess

Breman, Thomas

  1654-1655   Gloucester
  Burgess

Brent, George

  1688   Stafford
  Burgess

Brereton, Thomas

  1682   Northumberland
  Burgess

Brewer, John

  1658   Isle of Wight
  Burgess

Brewer, John

  bef.1616, d.1635   Warwick River
  Ancient Planter, Councillor

Brewster, Richard

  bef.1616, 1629-1644 Neck of Land
  Ancient Planter, Burgess James City

Bridger, Joseph

  1628-1686   Isle of Wight
  Councillor

Bristow, Robert

  d.by 1656   Mobjack Bay
  Landowner

Broadhurst, Walter

  1653   Northumberland
  Burgess

Brodnax, William

  1675-1717   Jamestowne Island
  Resident of Jamestowne

Brooks, Richard

  1642   Jamestowne Island
  Landowner

Brown, William

  1640, 1680-1682 James City, Surry
  Councillor, Burgess

Browne, Devereaux

| | 1663-1666 | Accomack |
| | Burgess | |

Browne, Henry

| | d.1661 | Surry |
| | Councillor | |

Browne, John

| | 1629 | Shirley Hundred |
| | Burgess | |

Browne, William

| | d.1704 | Surry |
| | Burgess | |

Browning, John

| | 1629-1632 | Elizabeth City |
| | Burgess | |

Buck, Richard, the Rev.

| | b.c.1582-d.by 1626 | Jamestowne Island |
| | Ancient Planter | Jamestowne |

Buckmaster, John

| | 1624 | Jamestowne Island |
| | Landowner | |

Buckner, John

| | 1682,1693 | Gloucester |
| | Burgess | |

Buckner, Thomas

| | 1698 | Gloucester |
| | Burgess | |

Buckner, William

| | d.1716 | York |
| | Burgess | |

Bullock, Hugh

| | d.1637 | England |
| | Councillor | York |

Burditt, William

| | bef.1616, 1639 | Accomack |
| | Ancient Planter, Burgess | |

Burges, Thomas

| | 1628-1630 | Warrascoyack |
| | Burgess | |

Burland, John
1628	Plantations Over the Water	
Burgess		

Burnham, John
1676-1680		Middlesex
Burgess		

Burnham, Rowland
1644-1649		York
Burgess		

Burroughs, Benoni
1695-1699		Princess Anne
Burgess		

Burroughs, Christopher
1645-1646, 1652		Lower Norfolk
Burgess		

Burrowes, Charles
1652		Lower Norfolk
Burgess		

Burwell, Edward
1579-1626	Huntingdonshire, England
Member Virginia Company	

Burwell, Lewis
1652-1710		York
Burgess		

Bush, John
d. 1624		Elizabeth City
Muster 1623/4		

Bushopp, John
1652, 1653		Charles City
Burgess		

Bushrod, Thomas
1659-1660		York
Burgess		

Butler, William
1642, 1653, 1658,		James City, Surry
Burgess		

Byrd, William, I
1652-1704		Charles City
Councillor		

C

Calthrope, Christopher
    1605-c.1662   York
    Burgess

Calvert, George
    1578/9-1632   London, England
    Stockholder Virginia Company

Canfield, Robert
    1676   Surry
    Burgess

Cant, David
    1660-1662   Gloucester
    Burgess

Cant, John
    1693   Middlesex
    Burgess

Carsley, Henry
    d.by 1635   Northampton
    Muster of 1624/5

Carter, Edward
    1658-1659   Upper Norfolk
    Burgess

Carter, John
    1620-1669   Lancaster
    Councillor

Carter, Robert (King)
    1662-1732   Lancaster
    Burgess, Councillor

Carter, William
    b.1600-d.by 1655   England
    Muster 1624/5   Surry

Carver, William
    1665-1669   Lower Norfolk
    Burgess

Cary, Miles
    1620-1667   Warwick
    Burgess, Councillor

Cary, William
| | 1693-1712 | Warwick |
| | Burgess | |

Castle, Robert
| | 1662 | Jamestowne Island |
| | Landowner | |

Catchmaid, George
| | 1661-1676 | Nansemond |
| | Burgess | |

Catlett, John
| | c.1658-1724 | Essex |
| | Burgess | |

Caufield, William
| | 1661-1662 | Surry |
| | Burgess | |

Caufleld, Robert
| | 1676 | Surry |
| | Burgess | |

Caulthropp, Christopher
| | 1645 | Elizabeth City |
| | Burgess | |

Causey, Thomas
| | 1640 | Martin's Hundred |
| | Burgess | |

Cawsey, Nathaniel
| | bef.1616, 1624-1625 | Charles City |
| | Ancient Planter, Burgess | |

Ceely, Thomas
| | 1629, 1630 | Warwicke River |
| | Burgess | Denby |

Ceney, Henry
| | 1630, 1632, 1633, | Glebe Land |
| | Burgess | Archer's Hope |

Challis, Edward
| | 1642 | Jamestowne Island |
| | Landowner | |

Chamberlain, Thomas
| | 1695-1696 | Charles City |
| | Burgess | |

Chamberlaine, Francis
    1625   Elizabeth City
    Burgess
Champion, William
    1677   Jamestowne Island
    Landowner
Chandler, John
    bef.1616, 1645-1649   Elizabeth City
    Ancient Planter, Burgess   Lower Norfolk
Chaplaine, Isaack
    bef.1616, 1624-1625   Charles City
    Ancient Planter, Burgess
Chapman, William
    1646   Jamestowne Island
    Landowner
Charlton, Stephen
    1645-1652   Northampton
    Burgess
Cheesman, Edmund
    1652   York
    Justice
Cheesman, John
    1643, 1652   York
    Burgess, Councillor
Cheesman, Thomas
    1685-1686   York
    Burgess
Chew, John
    1624, 1652   Jamestowne Island
    Landowner, Burgess   York
Chicheley, Henry, Sir
    1656, 1670-1683   Lancaster
    Burgess, Councillor
Chiles, Walter I
    1638-d.1658   Charles City
    Landowner   Black Point
    Councillor   Jamestowne Island
Chiles, Walter II
    1645-d.1671   Kemp House
    Landowner, Burgess   Jamestowne

Chiles, Susanna

    c.1670-c.1673   Jamestowne
    Landowner

Chilton, Edward

    1619,1680-1691   Jamestowne Island
    Landowner, Attorney General

Chudleigh, James

    1690   Jamestowne Island
    Landowner

Church, Richard

    1676, 1699, d.1706   Norfolk
    Burgess

Churchill, William

    1649-1711   Middlesex
    Burgess, Councillor

Claiborne, William I

    1621-bef.1679   Archer's Hope
    Surveyor, Ancient Planter
    Councillor, Treasurer, Secretary of State

Clarke, Richard

    1646   Jamestowne Island
    Landowner

Clause, Phettiplace

    bef.1616, 1629-1632   Mulberry Island
    Ancient Planter, Burgess   Water's Creek

Clay, John

    1587-d.by 1655   Charles City
    Ancient Planter

Clayton, Thomas

    1682   James City
    Burgess

Clements, Elizabeth (Fuller) see also Mrs. Ralph Hamor
    1617-widow of Jeffery Clements

Clements, Francis

    c.1685-d.1721   Surry
    Burgess

Clements, Jeremy

    1617-d. by 1657   Jamestowne, Surry
    Burgess

Cobb, Joseph

	1613-1654	Elizabeth City
	Muster of 1624/5	

Cocke, James

	1697-1699	Henrico
	Burgess	

Cocke, Richard

	1644, 1654-1655	Henrico
	Burgess	

Cocke, Thomas

	1662-1698-1699	Henrico
	Burgess	

Cocke, William

	1646	Henrico
	Burgess	

Cockerham, William

	1662-65	Surry
	Burgess	

Codd, St. Leger

	1680-1682, 1684	Northumberland
	Burgess	Lancaster

Cole, William

	1637-1713/14	Warwick
	Councillor	

Collclough, George

	1659	Northumberland
	Burgess	

Colston, William

	1691-1698	Rappahannock
	Burgess	Richmond

Coltrop, Christopher

	1645-1646	York
	Burgess	

Coogan, Daniell

	1642	Upper Norfolk
	Burgess	

Cooke, Mordecai

	1695-1696, 1699	Gloucester
	Burgess	

Cooke, Thomas
        1635-1637   Jamestowne Island
        Clerk of Council of State

Cooper, George
        1692, 1699   Northumberland
        Burgess

Corbin, Gawin
        1698, 1699   Middlesex
        Burgess

Corbin, Henry
        1629-1660, 1675   Lancaster
        Burgess, Councillor

Corker, John
        1632-1633, 1640, 1645   Jamestowne Island
        Landowner, Burgess, Clerk

Corker, William
        1658   James City
        Burgess

CortsenStam, Arent
        1638   Jamestowne Island
        Landowner

CortsenStam, Derrick
        1638   Jamestowne Island
        Landowner

Costnol, William
        1699   Richmond
        Burgess

Cotton, William, the Rev.
        w.p.1646   Accomack
        Anglican Minister

Cowles, Thomas
        1698   James City
        Burgess

Cowlinge, Christopher
        1630   Jamestowne Island
        Councillor

Cox(e), William
        1610-d.by 1656   Henrico
        Ancient Planter, Muster of 1624/5

Coxe, Richard

| | 1632 | Weyanoke |
| | Burgess | |

Coytmore, Rowland

| | 1565-1626 | Wales |
| | Stockholder Virginia Company | |

Crafford, William

| | 1695-1696 | Norfolk |
| | Burgess | |

Craford, William

| | 1697 | New Kent |
| | Burgess | |

Crampe, Thomas

| | 1632 | James City |
| | Burgess | |

Crashaw, Rawleigh

| | 1624 | Elizabeth City |
| | Burgess | |

Craven, Richard

| | bef. 1616 | Merchant's Hope |
| | Ancient Planter, Muster 1623/4 | |

Crawford, David

| | d.1710 | New Kent |
| | Burgess | |

Crawford, William

| | 1688 | Lower Norfolk |
| | Burgess | |

Crew, Randall

| | 1640,1643-1644 | Upper Norfolk |
| | Burgess | Warwick |

Crewes, James

| | 1676 | Henrico |
| | Burgess | |

Crinden, Edward

| | 1628 | Shirley |
| | Burgess | |

Cripp, Zachary

| | 1629, 1633, 1640 | Stanley Hundred |
| | Burgess | |

Crosbies, Mr.

1653, 1663		Jamestowne Island
Landowner		

Croshaw, Joseph

c.1612-1667		York
Burgess		

Croshaw, Raleigh

bef. 1616, d.1624		Elizabeth City
Member Virginia Company		
Ancient Planter		

Crump, John

1654		Jamestowne Island
Landowner		

Crump, Thomas

d.by 1654		James City
Burgess		

Curle, Pasco

1692		Elizabeth City
Burgess		

Curtis, Thomas

b.c.1600-d.1662		Gloucester
Muster of 1624/25		

Custis, John, II

1680-1692, d.1696		Northampton
Councillor		

Custis, John, III

1685-86, 1693-1699, d.1714	Northampton
Burgess, Councillor		

Custis, William

c.1677		Accomack
Burgess		

D

Dade, Francis (see Smith, John)

1658		Warwick

Dale, Edward

c.1628-1695		Lancaster
Burgess		

Dale, Thomas, Sir

1611, 1612, 1624   Jamestowne Island
Landowner, High Marshall
Deputy Governor,
Councillor, Acting Governor

Davenant, William, Sir

1650   n.p.l.
Councillor

Davenport, John, the Rev.

1622   London
Member Virginia Company

Davis, James

d.1624/5   Plantations Over the Water
Ancient Planter, Muster of 1624/25

Davis, Thomas

1656-1658   Warwick
Burgess

Davis, Thomas

1619   Martin's Brandon
Burgess

Davis, William

1643, 1647-1648   James City
Burgess

Davison, Christopher

1621, 1621-1623   Jamestowne Island
Councillor, Secretary of State

Dawson, William

b.1599 d.c.1664   Isle of Wight
Muster of 1624/5

Death, Richard

1643, 1644   Isle of Wight
Burgess

DeLaMajor, Thomas

1628   Jamestowne Island
Landowner

Delke, Roger

1633, d.c.1635   Stanley Hundred
Muster of 1624/5, Burgess

Denson, William

1660-1662, d.1676   Nansemond
Burgess

Dew, Thomas

1642-d.c.1691   Nansemond
Burgess, Councillor

Digges, Dudley

1665-1710/11   Warwick
Burgess, Councillor

Digges, Dudley, Sir

c.1583-1639   Kent, England
Stockholder Virginia Company

Digges, Edward

1621-1675/6   York
Councillor, Governor

Digges, William

1661-1676   York
Burgess

Dilke, Clement

1624, 1625   Flowerdieu Hundred
Burgess   Piercey's Hundred

Dipnall, Thomas

1654-1655   James City
Burgess

Doe, Thomas

1629   Archer's Hope
Burgess

Donne, George

1637   n.p.l.
Councillor

Douglas, Edward

1644, 1646   Northampton
Burgess

Dowman, John

1625, 1629   Corporation of
Burgess   Elizabeth City

Downes, George

1632   Lower Parish of
Burgess   Elizabeth City

Downing, John

        1693   Northumberland
        Burgess

Dowse, Thomas

        bef.1616, 1619   Henrico
        Ancient Planter, Burgess

Drummond, Sarah

        1662   Jamestowne Island
        Landowner

Drummond, William

        d.1676/7   Jamestowne Island
        Governor

Dudley, Robert

        1685-1699   Middlesex
        Burgess

Due, Thomas

        1652   Nansemond
        Burgess

Duke, Henry

        1691-1699, d.1713/14   James City
        Burgess, Councillor

Dunston, John

        1649   James City
        Burgess

E

Edloe, Matthew

        d.1668   James City
        Burgess

Edmundson, Thomas

        1693, 1696-1697   Essex
        Burgess

Edwards, William

        1693   James City
        Burgess

Edwards, William

        1615-1673   Surry
        Burgess

Elay, Lancelot

1653, 1663		Jamestowne Island
Landowner		

Elliot, Anthony

1647-1648	Elizabeth City, Lancaster	
1657-1658	Middlesex, Gloucester	
Burgess, Councillor		

Elliott, David

1663	Jamestowne Island
Landowner	

Ellis, David

1653	Jamestowne Island
Landowner	

Ellyson, Robert, Dr.

1644, 1655-1656. d.1666	James City
Burgess	

Emerson, Ellis

1625	Martin's Hundred
Burgess	

Emerson, William

1633	Weyanoke
Burgess	

English, John

1659, d.1678	Isle of Wight
Burgess	

English, William

1628-1659	Elizabeth City, Isle of Wight
Burgess	

Eppes, Francis, I

1597-1655	Charles City
Councillor	

Evans, Robert

1620, 1643	Jamestowne Island
Landowner	

Evelyn, Robert

1637	n.p.l.
Councillor	

Eyre, Robert

1646, 1647-1648	Lower Norfolk
Burgess	

F

Fairfax, William

    bef.1616, 1620   Jamestowne Island
    Ancient Planter, Landowner

Fantlaroy, Moore

    1645-1676   Upper Norfolk, Lancaster
    Burgess   Rappahannock

Fareley/Farley, Thomas

    1628-1634   Archer's Hope, Martin's
    Burgess   & Harrop's Plantations

Farlowe, Thomas

    1630   Archer's Hope
    Burgess

Farmer, Thomas

    bef.1616, 1630   Neck of Land
    Ancient Planter, Burgess

Farrar, John

    1680-1684   Henrico
    Burgess

Farrar, William

    d.1637   Charles City
    Councillor

Fauntleroy, Moore

    1644-d.c.1664   Rappahannock
    Burgess   Lancaster

Fawcett, Thomas

    1629   Martin's Hundred
    Burgess

Fawdone, George

    1646   Isle of Wight
    Burgess

Feild, Peter

    c.1647-1708   Henrico
    Burgess

Felgate, Robert

    1629, 1630   Plantations Other
    Burgess   Side of the Water

Ferrar, William	1661-1676 Burgess	Henrico
Filmer, Henry	d. after 1676 Burgess	Warwick
Filmer, Henry	1643 Burgess	James City
Finch, Henry	1630 Councillor	n.p.l.
Fisher, John	d.1639 Eastern Shore Census 1623/4	Accomack
Fitchett, John	1690 Landowner	Jamestowne Island
Fitzhugh, William	1677-1693 Burgess	Stafford
Fleet, Elizabeth	1655 Landowner	Jamestowne Island
Fleete, Henry	d.1660/61 Burgess	Lancaster
Fleete, William	b.1576-d.Jul 1620 Member Virginia Company	n.p.l.
Fletcher, George	1652, 1653 Burgess	Northumberland
Flint, Richard	1693 Burgess	Northumberland
Flint, Thomas	1629-1648 Burgess	Warwick River

Flood/Fludd, John

	bef.1616, d.1658	Surry
	Ancient Planter	
	Muster of 1624/5, Burgess	

Flynt, Thomas

| | 1632-1633 | Mulberry Island |
| | Burgess | Stanley Hundred, Denby |

Foliott, Edward

| | b.1610- d.1690 | England, York |
| | Minister | Hampton Parish |

Follis, Thomas

| | 1642 | James City |
| | Burgess | |

Ford, Richard

| | 1660 | James City |
| | Burgess | |

Fossett, Thomas

| | 1630 | Martin's Hundred |
| | Burgess | |

Foster, Joseph

| | 1684-1695-1696 | New Kent |
| | Burgess | |

Foster, Richard

| | 1656, 1658 | Lower Norfolk |
| | Burgess | |

Foulke, Thomas

| | 1659-1676 | James City, Westmoreland |
| | Burgess | |

Fowden, George

| | 1653 | Isle of Wight |
| | Burgess | |

Fowke, Gerrard

| | 1661-1676 | Westmoreland |
| | Burgess | |

Fowler, Bartholomew

| | 1699 | Jamestowne Island |
| | Attorney General | |

Fowler, Francis

| | 1642 | James City |
| | Burgess | |

Fox, David
                1677-1693   Lancaster
                Burgess
Foxcroft, Isaac
                1677, 1685-1686   Northampton
                Burgess
Francis, Lord Howard of Effingham
                1687   Jamestowne Island
                Lieutenant Governor
Francis, Thomas
                1658   Upper Norfolk
                Burgess
Franklin, Fardinand
                1642   James City
                Burgess
Freeman, Bridges
                1624-d.c.1663   James City
                Burgess, Councillor
Fulcher, John
                1677, 1690   Jamestowne Island
                Landowner
Fulford, Francis
                1642   Henrico
                Burgess

G

Gaither, John
                d.after 1666   Lower Norfolk
                Muster of 1624/5
Gascoygne/Gaskins, Thomas
                1636-1665   Northumberland
                Muster of 1624/5
Gates, Thomas, Sir
                1610, 1611   Jamestowne Island
                Ancient Planter
                Councillor, Acting Governor
George, John
                1647-1658, d.1678   Isle of Wight
                Burgess

Gibbes, John

1619   Ward's Plantation
Burgess

Gill, Stephen

1652   York
Burgess

Godfrey, Mathew

1699   Norfolk
Burgess

Godwin, Thomas

1654-1693   Nansemond
Burgess, Speaker of House of Burgesses

Gogh, Mathew

1642   Henrico
Burgess

Gooch, William

1654-1655   York
Burgess, Councillor

Goodrich, Charles

1695-1698   Charles City
Burgess

Goodrich, John

1695-1696   Isle of Wight
Burgess

Goodwin, James

1658, d.1679   York
Burgess

Goodwyn, Thomas

1659   Upper Norfolk
Burgess

Gookin, Daniel

b.1582-d.1632   Newport News
Stockholder Virginia Company

Gookin, John

1640   Upper Norfolk
Burgess

Gosnold, Bartholomew
        b.1571   Suffolk, England
        d. Aug. 1607   Jamestowne
        Organized Virginia Company
        Vice-Admiral of three ships to Virginia
        First Councillor

Gouge, William
        1652   York
        Burgess

Gough, Matthew
        1643, 1644   Henrico
        Burgess

Gough, William
        1699   King and Queen
        Burgess

Gouiston, Lyonell
        1632, 1633   York
        Burgess

Goulding, Thomas
        1638   Jamestowne Island
        Landowner

Gouldman, Thomas
        1680-1682   Rappahannock
        Burgess

Gower, Abel
        1679   Henrico
        Burgess

Graves, Thomas
        c.1570-d.1635/36   Accomack
        Member of Virginia Company
        Ancient Planter, Burgess

Gray, Francis
        1661-1676   Charles City
        Burgess

Gray, Thomas
        bef. 1616, d.c.1658   Jamestowne Island
        Ancient Planter, Muster 1624/5   Surry

Grayes, Thomas
        1632   Accomack
        Burgess

Gregory, Richard

1698	King and Queen
Burgess	

Gregson, Thomas

1698	Essex
Burgess	

Grendon, Edward

bef.1616, d.1628	Jamestowne Island
Ancient Planter, Landowner	

Grendon, Thomas, Sr.

1633, d.1680	Smith's Mount, Hog Island
Burgess	d. London England

Griffith, Edward

1660, 1661-1676	Warwick
Burgess	

Grubb, John

1620	Jamestowne Island
Landowner	

Gurganey, Edward

bef.1616, 1619	Argall's Gift
Ancient Planter, Burgess	

Gwillen, George

1661-1676	Nansemond
Burgess	

Gwyn, Hugh

1640-1652	Charles River, York
Burgess	Gloucester

Gyles, John

1695-1699	Isle of Wight
Burgess	

H

Hackett, Thomas

1653	Lancaster
Burgess	

Hallom, Robert

1620-d.by 1638	Charles City
Muster of 1623/4, 1624/5	

58

Ham, Jeremy
               1658   York
               Burgess

Hamlyn, Stephen
               1654-1655-1676   Charles City
               Burgess

Hammond, John
               1652   Isle of Wight
               Burgess

Hammond, Manwaring
               1660   New Kent
               Burgess, Councillor

Hamor, Elizabeth Fuller Clements
               1617, d.c.1630   James Cittie
               m.(2) Ralph Hamor c.1620
               m.(3) Capt. Tobias Felgate 1627/28
               Muster of 1624/1625

Hamor, Ralph
               1609-1626   Jamestowne Island
               Member of Virginia Company
               Landowner, Councillor
               Secretary of Colony

Hampton, Thomas
               1639, 1664   Jamestowne Island
               Member of the Virginia Company, Burgess

Hampton, William
               1620, d.c.1652   Gloucester
               Muster of 1624/5

Handy, George
               1649   Isle of Wight
               Burgess

Haney/Haynie, John
               1624-1697   Northumberland
               Burgess

Hardde, George
               1642, 1652   Isle of Wight
               Burgess

Hardidge, William
               1680-1693   Westmoreland
               Burgess

Hardin, George

1644, 1645-1646		Isle of Wight
Burgess		

Harlowe, John

1659		Warwick
Burgess		

Harmanson, Thomas

1688, 1691-1692		Northampton
Burgess		

Harmar, Charles

1632		Accomack
Burgess		

Harmer, Ambrose

1637, 1645, 1646		James City
Burgess, Councillor		
Speaker of House		

Harris, Adria

b.1602-d.c.1626		Neck of Land
Muster of 1624/5		Charles Cittie

Harris, John

1628, 1629, 1630		Shirley Hundred
Burgess		

Harris, Thomas

1611-d.c.1649	Neck of Land, Henrico	
Ancient Planter		
Muster of 1624/5, Burgess		

Harris, William

1652-1658		Henrico
Burgess		

Harris, William, Sr.

c.1628, d.1658		Jamestowne Island
Landowner		

Harris, William, Jr.

1658		Jamestowne Island
Landowner		

Harrison, Benjamin

1677-1698, 1698-1710		Surry
Burgess, Councillor		

Harrison, Benjamin		
	1642, d.1646	James City
	Burgess	
Harrison, Nathaniel		
	1699	Surry
	Burgess	
Hart, Samuel		
	1655	Jamestowne Island
	Landowner	
Hartwell, Henry		
	1684-1692	Jamestowne Island
	Landowner, Burgess, Councillor	
Hartwell, Henry		
	1619	n.p.l.
	Clerk	
Harvey, John Sir		
	1624-1636	Jamestowne Island
	Landowner, Councillor, Governor	
Harwood, Humphrey		
	1685-1686, 1693	Warwick
	Burgess	
Harwood, Thomas		
	1622, d.1652	Warwick
	Burgess, Councillor	
Harwood, William		
	1628	Martin's Hundred
	Burgess	
Hatcher, William		
	1644-1659	Henrico
	Burgess	
Hawkins, Thomas		
	1633	Denby
	Burgess	
Hawley, Jerome		
	1636, 1637-1639	n.p.l.
	Treasurer, Councillor	
Hay, William		
	1658, 1659	York
	Burgess	

Hayes, Robert

	1638	Lower Norfolk
	Burgess	

Haynes, Thomas

	1661-1676	Lancaster
	Burgess	

Hayney, Richard

	1695-1698	Northumberland
	Burgess	

Hayrick, Thomas

	1630	Elizabeth City
	Burgess	

Hayward/Howard, John

	c.1618-1660	York
	Burgess	

Hayward, Samuel

	1685-1686	Stafford
	Burgess	

Heale, George

	d.1698	Lancaster
	Burgess	

Henley, Reynold

	d.c.1694	Jamestowne Island
	Landowner	

Heyrick, Thomas

	1644	Warwick
	Burgess	

Heyricke, Henry

	1645	Warwick
	Burgess	

Higginson, Humphrey

	1641	James City
	Councillor	

Hill, Edward, Sr.

	1644-1660, d.c.1663	Charles City
	Councillor	Shirley
	Speaker of House of Burgesses	

Hill, Edward, Jr.

	1684, 1691-d.1700	Shirley
	Burgess, Councillor	Charles City
	Speaker of House of Burgesses	

Hill, John

| | 1639-1652 | Lower Norfolk |
| | Burgess | |

Hill, Nicholas

| | 1661-1676 | Isle of Wight |
| | Burgess | |

Hill, Richard

| | 1661-1676 | Isle of Wight |
| | Burgess | |

Hill, Thomas

| | 1642 | James City |
| | Burgess | |

Hinton, Thomas, Sr.

| | b.1575-d.1635 | n.p.l. |
| | Councillor | |

Hobbs, Francis

| | 1654-1655 | Isle of Wight |
| | Burgess | |

Hobson, John

| | 1636, 1637 | New Towne |
| | Councillor | |

Hockaday, William

| | 1653 | York |
| | Burgess | |

Hoddin, John

| | 1643 | Elizabeth City |
| | Burgess | |

Hodges, Thomas

| | 1693, 1696-1697 | Norfolk |
| | Burgess | |

Hooe/Hoe, Rice

| | b.1598-d.1665 | West & Shirley Hundred |
| | In Virginia 1623/24, Burgess | |

Holden, John

| | 1644 | Elizabeth City |
| | Burgess | |

Holder, Richard		
	1673 Landowner	Jamestowne Island
Holland, Gabriel		
	1624 Burgess	College Lands
Holland, John		
	1654-1655 Burgess	Westmoreland
Holliday, Anthony		
	1693-1699 Burgess	Isle of Wight
Holmewood, John		
	1656 Burgess	Charles City
Holt, Randall		
	1607/8-1639 Muster of 1624/5	James City
Holt, Robert		
	1656, 1661-1676 Burgess	James City
Holt, Thomas		
	1699, d.1731 Burgess	Surry
Hone, Theophilus		
	d.c.1679 Burgess	James City
Hooke, Francis		
	1637 Councillor	Elizabeth City
Hooker, William		
	1657-1667 Landowner	Jamestowne Island
Hopkins, Stephen		
	c.1610 Resident (brief)	Jamestowne
Horsey, Stephen		
	1653 Burgess	Northampton

Horsmenden, Warham
| | 1657-d.1691 | Charles City |
| | Burgess, Councillor | |

Horton, Thomas
	b.1555-d.1620	England
	Member of Guild	
	Stockholder Virginia Company	

Horwood, William
| | 1625 | Martin's Hundred |
| | Burgess | |

Hoskins, Anthony
| | 1652 | Northampton |
| | Burgess | |

Hoskins, Bartholemew
| | bef.1616, 1649-1656 | Lower Norfolk |
| | Ancient Planter, Burgess | |

Hough, Francis
| | 1633 | Nutmegg Quarter |
| | Burgess | |

Howe, John
| | 1632, 1633 | Accomack |
| | Burgess | |

Hubbard, Robert
| | 1691-1697 | Warwick |
| | Burgess | |

Huberd, Robert
| | 1649-1654 | n.p.l. |
| | Clerk | |

Hutt, Nathaniel
| | 1624 | Jamestowne Island |
| | Landowner | |

Hull, Peter
| | 1644 | Isle of Wight |
| | Burgess | |

Hunt, Thomas
| | 1655, 1680-1682 | Jamestowne Island |
| | Landowner, Burgess | Northampton |

Hutchinson, Robert
| | 1642-1648 | Jamestowne Island |
| | Landowner, Burgess | James City |

Hutchyson, William
>1632 Warrascoyack
>Burgess

I

Iversonn, Abraham
>1653 Gloucester
>Burgess

J

Jackson, John
>1619-1632 Martin's Hundred
>Landowner Jamestowne Island

James, Richard
>1655-1690 Jamestowne Island
>Landowner

Jaquelin, Edward
>1668-1739 Jamestowne
>Resident

Jarvis, Thomas
>1680-1682 Elizabeth City
>Burgess

Jefferson, John
>1619 Flowerdieu Hundred
>Burgess

Jeffreys, Herbert
>1677 Jamestowne Island
>Lieutenant Governor

Jenifer, Daniel
>1680-1693 Accomack
>Burgess

Jenings, Edmund
>1680-1691, 1699 Ripon Hall, York
>Attorney General, Councillor

Jenings, Peter
>1660-1676 Gloucester
>Burgess, Attorney General, Councillor

Jenkins, Henry
1680-1697   York, Elizabeth City
Burgess

Johns, Robert
1638   Jamestowne Island
Landowner

Johnson, Jacob
1693   Princess Anne
Burgess

Johnson, John
bef.1616, 1624   Jamestowne Island
Ancient Planter, Landowner

Johnson, John, Jr.
1655, 1659   Jamestowne Island
Landowner

Johnson, Joseph
1640   Charles City
Burgess

Johnson, Richard
1696   King and Queen
Councillor

Johnson, Thomas
1645-1655   Northampton
Burgess

Jones, Anthony
1640, 1643   Isle of Wight
Burgess

Jones, Rowland
1674-1688   York
Minister

Jones, William (see Pinke, William)
1624

Jones, William
1652-1693   Northampton
Burgess

Jordan, George
1644-1676   Surry
Burgess, Attorney General

Jordan, John

        1695-1696   Westmoreland
        Burgess

Jordan, Samuel

        bef.1616, 1619, d.by 1623   Charles City
        Ancient Planter, Burgess

Jordan, Sisley/Cicely

        1611, d.c.1637   Henrico
        Ancient Planter, m. (1) Samuel Jordan
        m. (2) William Farrar

Jordan, Thomas

        b.1661, 1696-1697   Nansemond
        Burgess

Jordan, Thomas

        d.by 1644   Isle of Wight
        Muster of 1624/5, Burgess

Jordayne, Thomas

        1646   James City
        Burgess

Jorden, George

        1644, 1647-1648   James City
        Burgess

Jorden, Thomas

        1628-1632   Warrascoyack
        Burgess

K

Kearney, Barnaby

        1684   Nansemond
        Burgess

Keeton, John

        1698   Nansemond
        Burgess

Kemp, Matthew

        1683   Gloucester
        Burgess, Councillor

Kemp, Richard

        1634, 1635-1649   James City
        Councillor, Governor
        Secretary of State

Kempe, William		
	1630	Elizabeth City
	Burgess	
Kendall, George		
	1607	Jamestowne Island
	Councillor	
Kendall, William		
	d.1686	Northampton
	Burgess	
Kenner, Richard		
	c.1640-c.1687	Northumberland
	Burgess	
Kenner, Rodham		
	1696-1697, 1699	Northumberland
	Burgess	
Kennon, Richard		
	1688	Northumberland
	Burgess	
Kennon, Richard		
	1696	Henrico
	Burgess	
Key, Thomas		
	bef.1616, 1630	Denby
	Ancient Planter, Burgess	
Kingsmill, Richard		
	1624-1629	James City
	Burgess	
Kingston, Thomas		
	bef.1616, 1629	Martin's Hundred
	Ancient Planter, Burgess	
Kirkman, Francis		
	1619	n.p.l.
	Clerk	
Knight, Mr.		
	1643	Jamestowne Island
	Landowner	
Knight, Peter		
	1658-1686	Northumberland
	Burgess	Gloucester

Knott, James

| | d.1653 | Surry, Maryland |
| | Muster of 1624/5 | |

Knowles, John

| | 1660-1690 | Jamestowne Island |
| | Landowner, Burgess | Lower Norfolk |

L

Lambert, Thomas

| | 1647-1658 | Lower Norfolk |
| | Burgess | |

Lane, ———

| | 1693 | King and Queen |
| | Burgess | |

Langhorne, John

| | 1680-1682 | Warwick |
| | Burgess | |

Langley, Ralph

| | 1656 | York |
| | Burgess | |

Langston, John

| | 1680-1682 | New Kent |
| | Burgess | |

Lapworth, Michael

| | 1621 | n.p.l. |
| | Councillor | |

Lawne, Christophor

| | 1619 | Lawne's Plantation |
| | Burgess | |

Lawrence, Richard

| | 1661-1676, 1683 | Jamestowne Island |
| | Landowner, Burgess | Lower Norfolk |

Lawson, Anthony

| | 1680-1692 | Lower Norfolk |
| | Burgess | |

Lear, John

| | 1661-1683 | Nansemond |
| | Burgess, Councillor | |

Lear, Thomas

1685-1693 Nansemond
Burgess

Ledford, Matthew, the Rev.

b.1663, d.1692/3 England
Minister, Christ Church Middlesex

Lee, Hugh

1651-1652 Northumberland
Burgess

Lee, Hancock

1688, 1698 Northumberland
Burgess

Lee, Henry

1652, d.by 1657 York
Burgess

Lee, John

1661-1676 Westmoreland
Burgess

Lee, Richard

1640-1677 York, Westmoreland
Burgess, Clerk of Grand Assembly

Lee, Richard

1651, 1660-1664 Northumberland
Councillor

Lee, Richard, II

1661-1676 Mt. Pleasant, Westmoreland
Burgess, Councillor

Leech, Mr.

1621 n.p.l.
Councillor

Leigh, Francis

1676 n.p.l.
Councillor

Leigh, William

1654-1704 King and Queen
Burgess New Kent

Lewis, William

1691-1692 James City
Burgess

Llewellyn, Daniel
               1646, d.1664   Charles City
               Burgess

Lightfoot, John
               d.1707   York
               Councillor

Ligon/Lyggon, Thomas
               1656, 1664-1679   Henrico
               Burgess

Littlepage, Richard
               1685-1686   New Kent
               Burgess

Littleton, Nathaniel
               d.1654   Northampton
               Councillor

Littleton, Southey
               1661-1676, 1677   Accomack
               Burgess

Lloyd/Loyd, Cornelius
               1645-1653   Lower Norfolk
               Burgess

Lloyd, Edward
               1645-1646, d.1696   Lower Norfolk
               Burgess

Lloyd, Thomas
               1698, 1699   Richmond
               Burgess

Lloyd, William
               1680-1682, 1685-1686   Rappahannock
               Burgess

Lobb, George
               1656   James City
               Burgess

Loveinge, Thomas
               1644-1658   James City
               Burgess

Lovelace, William, I, Sir
               b.1561-d.1629   England
               Member of Virginia Company

Lovelace, William, II, Sir
               b.1584-d.1628   Holland
               Member Virginia Company

Lucar, Thomas
               1658, 1661-1676   Rappahannock
               Burgess

Luddington, William
               1646   York
               Burgess

Ludlow, George
               1642   York
               Councillor

Ludlowe, George
               1642   Charles River
               Burgess

Ludwell, Philip
               1678, 1683-1694   Jamestowne Island
               Landowner, Councillor   James City
               Secretary of State

Ludwell, Philip, Jr.
               1696-1697   Jamestowne Island
               Burgess

Ludwell, Thomas
               1661-1678   Jamestowne Island
               Landowner, Councillor   James City
               Secretary of State

Luellin, Daniel
               1643, 1644   Henrico
               Burgess

Lunsford, Thomas, Sir
               1651   Rappahannock
               Councillor

Lupo, Albiano
               bef.1616, 1624   Kiccoughtan
               Ancient Planter, Councillor

Elizabeth Lupo, wife
               Ancient Planter   Elizabeth City

Lyddall, John
               1691-1692, 1693   New Kent
               Burgess

Lytefoote, John

   1624   Jamestowne Island
   Landowner

M

Macock/Maycocke, Samuel
   bef.1616, d.1622   n.p.l.
   Ancient Planter, Councillor

Macon, Gideon

   d.1702   New Kent
   Burgess

Madison, Isaac

   1624   West & Shirley Hundred
   Councillor, Burgess

Mainsfield, David

   1633   Martin's Hundred
   Burgess

Major, Edward

   1645-1646, 1652, 1653 Upper Norfolk
   Burgess, Speaker of House of Burgesses

Mansell, David

   1640 Johnson's Neck, Archer's Hope
   Burgess   Neck of Land

Mansill, Daniel

   1652   James City
   Burgess

Marble, George

   1663   Jamestowne Island
   Landowner

Marlott, Thomas

   1624   College Lands
   Burgess

Marshall, Robert

   1628   Jamestowne Island
   Landowner

Marshall, William

   1691-1692   Elizabeth City
   Burgess

Martiau, Nicholas		
	1620-1657 Muster of 1624/5, Burgess	York
Martin, John		
	1607-1652 Councillor, Burgess	Lower Norfolk
Mason, Francis		
	1613-1648 Ancient Planter, Muster of 1624/5	Lower Norfolk
Mason, George		
	1660-1716 Burgess	Stafford
Mason, James		
	1654-1655 Burgess	Surry
Mason, Lemuel		
	b.1629-d.1702, 1654-1693 Burgess	Lower Norfolk
Mason, Thomas		
	1696-1697, d.1711 Burgess	Norfolk
Mathew, Thomas		
	1676 Burgess	Stafford
Mathews, John		
	1680-1682, 1684 Burgess	Warwick
Mathews, Samuel		
	b.1629-d.1660, 1652-1654 Muster of 1624/5, Councillor, Burgess	Warwick
Matthews, Samuel II		
	1629-1660 Burgess, Councillor	Warwick
May, William		
	1661-1677 Landowner	Jamestowne Island
Meade, John		
	1619, 1642 Clerk, Clerk of Grand Assembly	n.p.l.

Meares, Thomas

| | 1602-1674 | Lower Norfolk |
| | Burgess | |

Meese, Henry

| | 1661-1680 | Stafford |
| | Burgess, Councillor | |

Mellin, William

| | 1653, 1658 | Northampton |
| | Burgess | |

Menefie, George

	1624-d.1645	Jamestowne Island
	Landowner	James City, Charles City
	Burgess, Councillor	

Meriwether, Nicholas

| | c.1631-1678 | Jamestowne |
| | Resident, Clerk of Council | Surry |

Michell, William

| | 1658 | Upper Norfolk |
| | Burgess | |

Middleton, David

| | 1620 | n.p.l. |
| | Councillor | |

Mihill, Edward

| | 1680-1682 | Elizabeth City |
| | Burgess | |

Mills, Henry

| | 1680-1682 | Nansemond |
| | Burgess | |

Milner, Francis

| | 1699 | Nansemond |
| | Burgess | |

Milner, Thomas

	1645-1699	Nansemond
	Clerk of General Assembly	
	Burgess, Speaker of House of Burgesses	

Minge, James

	1645-1684	Charles City
	Clerk, Burgess	
	Clerk of Grand Assembly	

Mole, Samuel

     1643   Jamestowne Island
     Landowner

Montague, Peter

     1621-1659   Lancaster
     Burgess

Moone, John

     1623-d.1655   Isle of Wight
     Burgess

More, John

     b.1588-d.c.1638   Elizabeth City
     Muster of 1624/5

Morgan, Francis

     1647-1648, 1652-1653   York
     Burgess

Morley, William

     1660   James City
     Burgess

Morris, George

     1680-1682   New Kent
     Burgess

Morrison, Richard

     1641   Elizabeth City
     Councillor

Moryson, Francis

     1643-1661   James City
     Councillor, Speaker of House of Burgesses
     Deputy Governor

Moseley, Arthur

     1649-1702   Lower Norfolk
     Burgess

Moseley, William

     1661-1697   Rappahannock, Essex
     Burgess   Lower Norfolk

Mottrom, John

     1645-1646, d.1655   Northumberland
     Burgess

Moyse, Theodore

     1629, 1630   Archer's Hope
     Burgess

N

Neale, Christopher
        1685-1686   Northumberland
        Burgess

Neale, John
        1639, 1640, 1642   Accomack
        Burgess

Newce, Thomas
        1620   n.p.l.
        Councillor

Newce, William, Sir
        1621   n.p.l.
        Councillor

Newell, David
        1681, 1690,   Jamestowne Island
        Landowner

Newell, Jonathan
        1690   Jamestowne Island
        Landowner

Newman, ———
        1693   Westmoreland
        Burgess

Newman, Alexander
        1696-1697   Richmond
        Burgess

Newport, Christopher
        1607   Jamestowne Island
        Councillor

Nicholson, Francis, Col.
        1661-1698   n.p.l.
        Lieutenant Governor

Nicholson, Francis, Sir
        1690   n.p.l.
        Councillor

Norsworthy, Tristram
        1640, d.c.1657   Upper Norfolk
        Burgess

Norton, John

   1638   Jamestowne Island
   Landowner

Norwood, Charles

   1654-1656   n.p.l.
   Clerk Grand Assembly

Norwood, Henry

   1660-1677   n.p.l.
   Treasurer

O

Offley, Robert

   b.1561-d.1625   London, England
   Stockholder Virginia Company

Oldis, Thomas

   1640   Elizabeth City
   Burgess

O'Neil, Grace

   1618-c.1682   Northampton
   Muster of 1624/5
   m.(1) Edward Waters
   m.(2) Obedience Robins

Osborne, John

   1643   Jamestowne Island
   Landowner

Osborne, Thomas

   1619, d.after 1667   Henrico
   Muster of 1624/5, Burgess

Ouldsworth, Mr.

   1621   Berkeley Hundred
   Councillor

Ousley/Owsley, Thomas

   1658-1700   Stafford
   Burgess

P

Pace, Isabella Smith

    1616-after 1628   Pace's Paines

    Ancient Planter   James City

    m.(2) William Perry, (3) George Menefie

Pace, Richard

    bef.1616, d.c.1623   Jamestowne

    Ancient Planter

Page, Francis

    1635-1688   York

    Clerk, Burgess

    Clerk of General Assembly

Page, John

    1627-1692   Middle Plantation, York

    Councillor

Page, Matthew

    1699   Timber Neck, Gloucester

    Councillor

Pagett, Anthony

    1629   Flowerdieu Hundred

    Burgess

Paine/Payne, Florentine

    1642, 1659   Elizabeth City

    Burgess

Palmer, Thomas

    1629-1630   Shirley Hundred

    Burgess

Parke, Daniel

    c.1628-1679   York

    Councillor

Parke, Daniel, II

    1692   York

    Councillor

Parker, William

    bef.1616, 1642   Upper Norfolk

    Ancient Planter, Burgess

Parry, William

    1636   Jamestowne Island

    Landowner

Passmore, Thomas
    1624, 1628, 1652   Jamestowne Island
    Landowner

Pate, John
    1670   Gloucester
    Councillor

Pate, Richard
    1653   Gloucester
    Burgess

Pate, Thomas
    1684   Gloucester
    Burgess

Paule, Thomas
    1643   Jamestowne Island
    Landowner

Paulett, Robert
    1621   n.p.l.
    Councillor

Paulett, Thomas
    1633   Westover, Flowerdieu Hundred
    Burgess

Pawlett, Thomas
    1619, 1628-1641   Argall's Gift
    Burgess, Councillor   Charles City

Peirce/Pierce, William, Capt.
    1610, 1625, 1645   Jamestowne Island
    Ancient Planter, Landowner
    Member of the Convention, Councillor

Peirsey, Abraham
    c.1616-1627/8   Weyanoke
    Stockholder Virginia Company
    Ancient Planter, Councillor

Peppet, Gilbert
    1625   Piercey's Hundred
    Burgess

Percy, George, Capt.
    1609-1611   Jamestowne Island
    President of Council, Deputy Governor

Perkins, William

        b.1580-d.1657   n.p.l.
        Guild Member,
        Stockholder Virginia Company

Perrott/Parrot, Richard, Sr.

        1677, 1684   Middlesex
        Burgess

Perry, Henry

        1652-1655   Charles City, James City
        Burgess, Councillor

Perry, Peter

        1688   Charles City
        Burgess

Perry, William

        bef.1616, d.1637   Paces's Paines
        Ancient Planter   Charles City
        Burgess, Councillor

Pettus, Thomas

        d.c.1661   James City
        Councillor

Peyton, Valentine

        1663-d.1664   Westmoreland
        Burgess

Phipps, John

        1656-1665   Jamestowne Island
        Burgess

Pierce, Alice (Bennett)

        c.1619-c.1642   Lawnes Creek
        Landowner

Pierce, William

        1680-1682, d.1702   Westmoreland
        Burgess

Pinkard, John

        d.1690   Lancaster
        Burgess

Pinke, William (alias William Jones)

        1624   Jamestowne Island
        Landowner

Pinkhorne, John

    1657, 1667   Jamestowne Island
    Landowner

Pitt, Robert

    d.1673   Isle of Wight
    Burgess

Pitt, Thomas

    1680-1682   Isle of Wight
    Burgess

Place, Rowland

    1675   n.p.l.
    Councillor

Pleasant, John

    1693   Henrico
    Burgess

Pocahontas/Matoaka

    d.1617   d. Gravesend, England
    Native American
    m. John Rolfe (see Rolfe entry)

Polentine, John

    1619   City of Henricus
    Burgess

Pollington, John

    1624   Martin's Hundred
    Burgess

Poole, Henry

    1647-1648   Elizabeth City
    Burgess

Popkton, William

    1628, 1629   Jourden's Journey
    Burgess

Porter, Joseph

    1661-1676   Lower Norfolk
    Burgess

Pory, John

    1619   Jamestowne Island
    Councillor, Secretary of State
    Speaker of House

Pott, Francis, Capt.

1640		Jamestowne Island
Landowner		

Pott, John, Dr.

1621-1628		Jamestowne Island
Landowner		James City
Governor, Councillor		

Pountis, John

1620		n.p.l.
Councillor		

Powel, James

1680-1682		Isle of Wight
Burgess		

Powel, John

1632, 1658-1676		Water's Creeke
Burgess		Elizabeth City

Powell, Nathaniel, Capt.

1619		Jamestowne Island
Senior Councillor		
Acting Governor		

Powell, William

bef.1616, 1619		James City
Burgess		

Poythres, Francis

1644-1649		Charles City
Burgess		Northumberland

Prescott, Edward

1661		Jamestowne Island
Landowner		

Presley, Peter

1661-1692		Northumberland
Burgess		

Presley, William

1647-1682		Northumberland
Burgess		

Price, Arthur

1645-1646		Elizabeth City, York
Burgess		

Price, John

	1611-d.1628	Neck of Land
	Ancient Planter	
	Muster of 1624/5, Burgess	

Price, Walter

| | 1628-1630 | Chaplain's Choice |
| | Burgess | |

Prince, Edward

| | 1645, 1645-1646, | Charles City |
| | Burgess | |

Pritchard, Thomas

| | 1656 | Gloucester |
| | Burgess | |

Pryor, William

| | 1640 | Charles River |
| | Burgess | |

Purefoy, Thomas

| | 1621-1639 | Elizabeth City |
| | Muster of 1624/5, Councillor | |

Pyland, James

| | 1652, 1659 | Isle of Wight |
| | Burgess | |

R

Rabley, Thomas

| | 1689 | Jamestowne Island |
| | Landowner | |

Radish, John

| | 1637 | Jamestowne Island |
| | Landowner | |

Ramsey, Edward

| | 1661-1676 | James City |
| | Burgess | |

Ramsey, Thomas

| | 1656, 1658 | Gloucester |
| | Burgess | |

Ramshawe, Thomas

| | 1632 | Warwick River |
| | Burgess | |

Randolph, Henry

1623-1673		Henrico
Clerk, House of Burgesses		

Randolph, William

1651-1711		Henrico
Councillor		

Ransom, Peter

1652		Elizabeth City
Burgess		

Ransom, James

1691-1699		Gloucester
Burgess		

Rashell, Humphrey

1628		James City, The Merchants
Burgess		

Ratcliffe, John, Capt.

1607		Jamestowne Island
President of Council		

Read, Edward

1680-1682		Accomack
Burgess		

Read, Robert

1688		York
Burgess		

Reade, George

1658-1671		York
Councillor		

Revell, Randall

1658		Northampton
Burgess		

Reynolds, Charles

1652		Isle of Wight
Burgess		

Reynolds, Christopher

1622-d.1654		Isle of Wight
Muster of 1624/5, Burgess		

Richards, Richard

1632-1642		James City
Burgess		

Richardson, John

| | 1691-1692, 1693 | Princess Anne |
| | Burgess | |

Ricks, Richard

| | 1660 | Jamestowne Island |
| | Landowner | |

Ridley, John

| | 1645, 1645-1646 | James City |
| | Burgess | |

Ridley, Peter

| | 1647-1648 | James City |
| | Burgess | |

Ring, Joseph

| | 1684, 1691-1693 | York |
| | Burgess | |

Robins, John

| | 1691-1692 | Elizabeth City |
| | Burgess | |

Robins, Obedience

| | b.1601-d.1662 | Northampton |
| | Councillor | |

Robinson, Christopher

| | 1645-1693 | Middlesex |
| | Councillor | |

Robinson, Tully

| | 1658-1723 | Accomack |
| | Burgess | |

Robinson, William

| | 1684-1696 | Lower Norfolk |
| | Burgess | |

Rodgers, Richard

| | 1693, d.1697 | Northumberland |
| | Burgess | |

Rogers, John

| | d.c.1684 | James City |
| | Burgess | |

Rolfe, John

| | b.1585-d.1622 | Jamestowne Island |
| | Ancient Planter, Councillor | |

Rookings, William

        b.1598-d.c.1647   James City
        Musters of 1623/4,1624/25

Roper, William

        1644   Northampton
        Burgess

Roscow, William

        1693-1699   Warwick
        Burgess

Rossingham, Edmund

        1619   Flowerdieu Hundred
        Burgess

Rowlston, Lionel

        1629   Elizabeth City
        Burgess

Royall, Joseph

        1622-by 1655/6   Charles City, Henrico
        Census of 1623/4, Muster of 1624/5

S

Sadler, Rowland

        1643   James City
        Burgess

St. Leger, Warham, Sir

        d.1631   County Kent, England
        Member Virginia Company

Salmon, Joseph

        1642   Isle of Wight
        Burgess

Sanders, Richard

        1642   Jamestowne Island
        Landowner

Sanderson, Edward

        1638   Jamestowne Island
        Landowner

Sandiford, John

        1691-1692   Lower Norfolk
        Burgess

Sandys, George
    1621-1625   Jamestowne
    Councillor, Treasurer

Sanford, Samuel
    1693   Accomack
    Burgess

Sargent, William
    1657, 1667   Jamestowne Island
    Landowner

Saunders, Roger
    1633   Accomack
    Burgess

Savage, John
    1661-1676   Northampton
    Burgess

Savage, Thomas
    1607/8-d.by 1633   Accomack
    Ancient Planter, Muster of 1624/5

Savin, Robert
    1629-1633   Warrascoyack
    Burgess

Sawyer, Francis
    1691-1693   Norfolk
    Burgess

Scarborough, Charles
    1680-1692   Accomack
    Councillor, Burgess

Scarburgh, Edmund, I
    b.1584-d.1635   Accomack
    Burgess

Scarburgh, Edmund, II
    b.1617-d.1671   Accomack
    Speaker of House of Burgesses
    Surveyor General

Scarlet, Martin
    1680-1696   Stafford
    Burgess

Scotchmore, Robert
    1630-1633   Martin's Hundred
    Burgess

Scott, John

    1698   Westmoreland
    Burgess

Scrivenor, Matthew

    1608   Jamestowne Island
    Councillor

Seawell, Henry

    1632-1640   Upper Elizabeth City
    Burgess   Lower Norfolk

Seely, Thomas

    1632   Warwick River
    Burgess

Senior/Scinior, John

    1652, 1654   Jamestowne Island
    Landowner

Seward, John

    1645-1646   Isle of Wight
    Burgess

Sharp, Samuel

    bef.1616, 1619-1629   Charles City
    Ancient Planter, Burgess

Sharp, William

    1611-d.by 1635/6   Henrico
    Member Virginia Company
    Ancient Planter, Burgess

Sharpless, Edward

    1619, 1624   n.p.l.
    Clerk, Clerk of General Assembly

Shelley, Walter

    1619   Smythe's Hundred
    Burgess

Shepherd, Baldwin

    1680-1682   Elizabeth City
    Burgess

Sheppard, John

    1644, 1652-d.1655   Elizabeth City
    Burgess   James City

Sheppard, Robert

    1646-1648, d.by 1654   James City
    Burgess

Sheppard, Thomas
    1633   Upper Parish Elizabeth City
    Burgess

Sheppey, Thomas
    1620-c.1655   Henrico
    Muster of 1624/5

Sherlock, James
    1619   n.p.l.
    Clerk

Sherman, Michael
    1693, 1696-1697   James City
    Burgess

Sherwood, William
    1677-1697   Jamestowne Island
    Landowner, Burgess   James City
    Attorney General

Sibsey, John
    1637-1640, d.1652   Lower Norfolk
    Burgess, Councillor   Elizabeth City

Sidney, John
    1644-1660   Lower Norfolk
    Burgess

Slaughter, John
    1650   Rappahannock
    Muster of 1624/5

Smith, Arthur
    b.1600-d.1645   Isle of Wight
    Census of 1623/4
    Muster of 1624/5, Burgess

Smith, Arthur
    1680-1692, d.1697   Isle of Wight
    Burgess

Smith, John
    1685-1692   Gloucester
    Burgess

Smith, John (alias Francis Dade)
    1658   Warwick
    Speaker of House of Burgesses

Smith, John, Captain

	1607-d.1631	Jamestowne Island
	Ancient Planter	d. London
	President of Council	

Smith, Lawrence

| | 1629-1700 | Gloucester |
| | Burgess | |

Smith, Nicholas

| | 1656-1676 | Isle of Wight |
| | Burgess | |

Smith, Richard

	1619-d.1659/60	James City
	Census of 1623/4	Northampton
	Muster of 1624/5	

Smith, Robert

| | 1663 | Brandon, Lancaster |
| | Councillor | Middlesex |

Smith, Roger

	1616, 1621, 1624	Jamestowne Island
	Landowner	
	Ancient Planter, Councillor	

Smith, Toby

| | 1643-1649 | Warwick, Upper Norfolk |
| | Burgess | Nansemond |

Smyth, John

| | 1628-1632 | Pace's Paines |
| | Burgess | |

Soane, Henry

	c.1622-1676	James City
	Burgess, Speaker of House	
	Speaker Grand Assembly	

Soane, William

| | 1695-1697 | Henrico |
| | Burgess | |

Somers, George, Sir

| | 1610 | n.p.l. |
| | Councillor | |

Southcot, Thomas

| | 1661-1676 | Charles City |
| | Burgess | |

Southerne, John		
	1619-1652	Jamestowne Island
	Landowner	James City
	Clerk, Burgess	
Sparrow, Charles		
	1645-1660	Charles City
	Burgess	
Speke, Thomas		
	1651-1652	Northumberland
	Burgess	
Spence, Alexander		
	1693-1699	Westmoreland
	Burgess	
Spencer, Nicholas		
	d.c.1689	Westmoreland
	Councillor	
Spencer, William		
	1607-l.1637	Jamestowne Island
	Ancient Planter, Landowner	
	Muster of 1624/5	
Spicer, Arthur		
	1685-1696	Rappahannock, Richmond
	Burgess	
Spier, John		
	1680-1682	Nansemond
	Burgess	
Spraggon, Radulph		
	1642	Jamestowne Island
	Landowner	
Stacy, Robert		
	1619	Martin's Brandon
	Burgess	
Stafferton, Peter		
	1640	Elizabeth City
	Burgess	
Stegg, Thomas I		
	d.1651/52	Charles City
	Councillor	

Stegg, Thomas, II

1664, 1667		Jamestowne Island
Councillor, Landowner		

Stephens, George

1645-1652		James City, Surry
Burgess		

Stephens, Richard

1623-d.c.1636		Jamestowne Island
Census 1623/4, Landowner		James City
Muster of 1624/1625		
Burgess, Councillor		

Stith, John

1638-1694	Charles City
Burgess	

Stone, John

d.1693	Rappahannock
Burgess	

Stone, Maximillian

1628	Hogg Island
Burgess	

Stoner, Alexander

1637	Jamestowne Island
Landowner	

Stoner, John

1634	n.p.l.
Councillor	

Story, Joshua

1691-1697	King and Queen
Burgess	

Stoughton, Samuel

1646-1655	Nansemond, Upper Norfolk
Burgess	

Strachey, William

c.1572-1611	England
Stockholder Virginia Company	
Secretary of the Colony	Jamestowne Island

Stratton, Joseph

1630-1632	Nutmegg Quarter
Burgess	Water's Creek

Strechley, John

| 1693, 1695-1696 | Lancaster |
| Burgess | |

Stretter, Edward

| 1656 | Nansemond |
| Burgess | |

Stringer, John

| 1659-1676 | Northampton |
| Burgess | |

Sully, Thomas

| 1624 | Jamestowne Island |
| Landowner | |

Swann, Alexander

| 1699 | Lancaster |
| Burgess | |

Swann, Samuel

| 1677-1693 | Surry |
| Burgess | |

Swann, Thomas

| 1616-1680 | Surry |
| Burgess, Councillor | |

Sweete, Robert

| 1628 | Elizabeth City |
| Burgess | |

T

Taberer, Thomas

| 1658, 1680-1682 | Isle of Wight |
| Burgess | |

Talbot, Ann

| 1657 | Jamestowne Island |
| Landowner | |

Taliaferro, John

| 1699, d.1720 | Essex |
| Burgess | |

Tatum, Nathaniel

| 1619-c.1676 | Charles City |
| Muster of 1624/5 | |

Tayler, Phillip

	1643	Northampton
	Burgess	

Tayloe, William

	1695-1710	Richmond
	Burgess	

Taylor, George

	1684	Rappahannock
	Burgess	

Taylor, John

	1693-1699	Charles City
	Burgess	

Taylor, Richard

	bef.1616, 1628	College Lands
	Ancient Planter, Burgess	

Taylor, Thomas

	bef.1616, d.c.1656	Warwick
	Ancient Planter, Burgess	

Taylor/Tayloe, William

	1651	York
	Councillor	

Thomas, Edward

	1693	Essex
	Burgess	

Thomas, Lord Culpeper

	1680	Jamestowne
	Governor	

Thomas, William

	1652, 1656	Surry
	Burgess	

Thompson, George

	1629	Elizabeth City
	Burgess	

Thompson, John

	1693-1697	Surry
	Burgess	

Thornbury, Thomas

	bef.1616, 1653	Elizabeth City
	Ancient Planter, Burgess	

Thoroughgood, Adam		
	1664-1670, d.1685	Lower Norfolk
	Burgess	
Thorowgood, Adam		
	1603-1640	Lower Norfolk
	Burgess, Councillor	
Thorowgood, John		
	1695-1699	Princess Anne
	Burgess	
Thorpe, George		
	1620	Berkeley Hundred
	Councillor	
Thorpe, Otto		
	1680-1682	York
	Burgess	
Thruston, Malachi		
	1661-1698	Lower Norfolk
	Burgess	Princess Anne
Tiler, Richard		
	1625	College Lands
	Burgess	
Tonstall, Edward		
	1640	Henrico
	Burgess	
Tooke/Tuke, James		
	1621-d.c.1662	Isle of Wight
	Burgess	
Townshend, Richard		
	1620-1651	Charles River, York
	Burgess, Councillor	
Tracy, William		
	1620, d.1621	Berkeley Hundred
	Councillor	
Trahorne, John		
	1630	Weyanoke
	Burgess	
Travers, Raleigh		
	1651-1676	Lancaster
	Burgess	

Travers, William

	1677	n.p.l.
	Speaker of House of Burgesses	

Traverse, Samuel

	1696-1697	Richmond
	Burgess	

Travis, Edward

	1637, 1653	Jamestowne Island
	Landowner, Burgess	James City

Travis, Edward, Jr.

	1663, 1677	Jamestowne Island
	Landowner	

Travis, Rebecca

	1677-1723	Jamestowne Island
	Resident	

Tree, Richard

	1627-1632	Jamestowne Island
	Landowner, Burgess	Hog Island

Trussell, John

	1622, 1651-1655	Northumberland
	Burgess	

Tuckar/Tucker, William

	bef.1616, 1619-1625	Elizabeth City
	Ancient Planter	Kecoughtan
	Councillor, Burgess	

Tucker, Daniel

	1619	n.p.l.
	Councillor	

Turner, Charles

	1680-1682	New Kent
	Burgess	

Twine, John

	1619	n.p.l.
	Clerk of General Assembly	

U

Underwood, William

	1652	Lancaster
	Burgess	

Upton, John		
	1630-1648	Warroscoyack
	Burgess	Isle of Wight
Usher, James		
	b.c.1595-d.c.1620	England, Henrico
Utie, John		
	d.1639	York
	Councillor	

V

Vassall, John		
	1548-1625	Essex County, England
	Virginia Company Stockholder	

W

Wade, Armiger		
	1656, d.1676	York
	Burgess	
Waidson, Thomas		
	1619	n.p.l.
	Clerk	
Waldoe, Richard		
	1608	n.p.l.
	Councillor	
Walker, John		
	c.1601-1671	Warwick
	Councillor	
Walker, Peter		
	1654-1656	Northampton
	Burgess	
Walker, Thomas		
	after 1683	Gloucester
	Burgess	
Wallings, George		
	1661-1676	Nansemond
	Burgess	
Walthall, Richard		
	b.c.1577-d.c.1625	England

Ware/Weire, John
    d.1678   Rappahannock
    Burgess

Wareham, John
    1632-1633   Mounts Bay
    Burgess   Martin's Hundred

Warde, John
    bef.1616, 1619   Ward's Plantation
    Burgess

Warne, Thomas
    1645-1646   James City
    Burgess

Warner, Augustine, I
    b.1611-d.1674   Warner Hall
    Councillor, Burgess   Gloucester
    Speaker of House of Burgesses

Warner, Augustine, II
    b.1642-d.1681, 1661-1677   Gloucester
    Speaker of House of Burgesses, Councillor

Warner, Austin
    1652   York
    Burgess

Warren, John
    1658-1676   Lower Norfolk
    Burgess

Warren, Thomas
    1659-1676, d.1670   Surry
    Burgess

Washbourne, John
    1693-1697   Accomack
    Burgess

Washer, Ensigne
    1619   Lawne's Plantation
    Burgess

Washington, John
    c.1634-1677   Westmoreland
    Burgess

Washington, Lawrence
    1684-1692   Westmoreland
    Burgess

Waters, Edward		
	c.1610-1630 Ancient Planter, Burgess	Elizabeth City
Waters, William		
	1654-1682 Burgess	Northampton
Waters, William		
	1693, 1695-1697 Burgess	Northampton
Watkins, Henry		
	1624 Burgess	Eastern Shore
Watts, Mathew		
	1695-1696 Burgess	Elizabeth City
Wattson, Abraham		
	1652-1655 Burgess	James City
Wattson, John		
	1643, 1644 Landowner	Jamestowne Island
Waugh, John		
	1699 Burgess	Stafford
Webb, Giles		
	d. after 1667 Burgess	Nansemond
Webb, Stephen		
	1643, 1644 Burgess	James City
Webb, Wingfeild		
	1654-1655 Burgess	Gloucester
Webster, Richard		
	1658, 1681 Landowner, Burgess	Jamestowne Island James City
Webster, Roger		
	1632 Burgess	Glebe, Archer's Hope

Weeks, Abraham

    1677-1684   Middlesex

    Burgess

Welbourne, Thomas

    1699   Accomack

    Burgess

Weld(e), Humphrey

    d.1610   n.p.l.

    Stockholder Virginia Company

Weldon, Poynes

    1695-1696   James City

    Burgess

Wells, Richard

    d.1667   Upper Norfolk

    Burgess

West, Anthony

    1622-1652   Northampton

    Muster of 1624/25

West, Francis

    1609, 1627-29, d.1634   Jamestowne

    Ancient Planter

    Councillor, Governor

West, John

    b.1638-1676, d.1703   Accomack

    Burgess

West, John

    b.1590-d.1659   West Point

    Burgess, Councillor

West, John

    b.1632, 1680-d.1691   New Kent

    Burgess

West, Thomas (Lord De La Warr)

    b.1577, 1610, d.1662   Jamestowne

    Governor, Captain General

Weston, Thomas

    1628   Kecoughtan

    Burgess

Westropp, John

    1644   Charles City

    Burgess

Wetherall, Robert
    1645-1646, 1652   James City
    Burgess

Weynman, Ferdinando, Sir
    1610   n.p.l.
    Councillor

Whitaker, Jabez
    1624, 1626-1628   Jamestowne Island
    Burgess, Councillor

Whitaker, Richard
    1680-1697   Warwick
    Burgess

Whitaker, Walter
    1661-1676   Middlesex
    Burgess

Whitaker, William
    1649-1659   Middlesex, James City
    Burgess, Councillor

Whitby, William
    1644, 1653   Warwick
    Burgess, Speaker of House of Burgesses

White, John
    1642   Jamestowne Island
    Landowner, Burgess   James City

White, William
    1680-1682   James City
    Burgess

Whiting, Henry
    b.c.1650-d.1728   Gloucester
    Burgess, Councillor

Whittbey, William
    1642-1655   Warwick River
    Burgess

Whittington, William
    1680-1682   Northampton
    Burgess

Wickham, William, the Rev.
    1619   n.p.l.
    Councillor

Wigg(s), William

	b.1608 - d.by 1654	Jamestowne Island
	Landowner, Surveyor	

Wight, John

	1695-1696	Nansemond
	Burgess	

Wilcocks, John

	1624	Eastern Shore
	Burgess	

Wilcox, John

	1656	Nansemond
	Burgess	

Wild, Daniel

	1661-1676	York
	Burgess	

Wilford, Thomas

	1651-1652	Northumberland
	Burgess	

Wilkins, John

	1618-1651	Northampton
	Muster of 1624/5, Burgess	

Wilkinson, John

	1633	Accomack
	Burgess	

Wilkinson, Thomas

	1655	Jamestowne Island
	Landowner	

Wilkinson, William

	1635-1650	Lynnhaven Parish
	Minister	Princess Anne

Willcox, John

	1658	Northampton
	Burgess	

Williamson, James

	1652	Lancaster
	Burgess	

Williamson, Robert, Dr.

	1662, d.1670	Isle of Wight
	Burgess	

Willis, Francis

    1652-1676   Gloucester, York
    Burgess, Councillor

Willoughby, Thomas

    1610-c.1657   Lower Norfolk
    Ancient Planter, Councillor

Wilson, James

    1698, d.1712   Norfolk
    Burgess

Wilson, William

    1684-1699   Elizabeth City
    Burgess

Windham, Edward

    1642, 1643   Lower Norfolk
    Burgess

Wingate, Roger

    1639, 1639-1641   n.p.l.
    Councillor, Treasurer

Wingfield, Edward Maria, Capt.   Jamestowne Island
    1607
    President of Council

Withers, John

    1691-1697   Stafford
    Burgess

Wood, Gen. Abraham

    1644-1657   Henrico, Charles City
    Burgess, Councillor

Wood, Percivall

    1628-1632   Archer's Hope
    Burgess   Martin's Hundred

Woodhouse, Henry

    d.1637   County Norfolk, England
    Stockholder Virginia Company

Woodhouse, Henry

    1607-1655   Lower Norfolk
    Burgess

Woodhouse, Thomas

    1655-1667   Jamestowne Island
    Landowner

Woodliffe, John

1652		Charles City
Burgess		

Woodson, John

1619-1644		Henrico
Muster of 1624/5		

Woodward, Christopher

1620, 1629, d.by 1650		Westover
Muster of 1624/5, Burgess		

Woodward, Henry

1625		Warrascoyack
Burgess		

Wooldridge, William

1644, 1658		Elizabeth City
Burgess		

Woory, Joseph

1684		Isle of Wight
Burgess		

Worleigh, George

1642		Charles River
Burgess		

Worlech, William

1660-1676		Elizabeth City
Burgess		

Worlich, William

1654-1655		Elizabeth City
Burgess		

Worloch, William

1649		Elizabeth City
Burgess		

Wormeley, Christopher

1637, 1643		York
Councillor		

Wormeley, Ralph I

1650-1651		York, Lancaster
Burgess, Councillor		Middlesex

Wormeley, Ralph II

1675-1701		n.p.l.
Burgess, Councillor		

Wyatt, Anthony
     1645-1656   Charles City
     Burgess

Wyatt, Francis, Sir
     1621-1626, 1640-1641   Jamestowne Island
     Landowner
     Governor, Councillor

Wyatt, Haute, the Rev.
     1594-1638   County Kent, England
     Resident   Jamestowne

Wyatt, Nicholas
     1661-1676   Charles City
     Burgess

Wynne, Peter
     1608   Jamestowne
     Councillor

Wynne, Robert
     c.1622-d.1675   Charles City
     Burgess, Grand Assembly
     Speaker of House of Burgesses

Wythe, Thomas
     1680-1682   Elizabeth City
     Burgess

Y

Yeardly, Francis
     1653   Lower Norfolk
     Burgess

Yeardley, Argoll
     b.1616-d.1655   Northampton
     Councillor

Yeardley, George, Sir
     1609-d.1627   Jamestowne Island
     Landowner, Deputy-Governor
     Governor, Captain-General of Virginia
     Councillor   Flowerdieu Hundred

Yeo, Hugh
     1661-1676   Accomack
     Burgess

Yeo, Lenard

| | 1645-1646, 1661-1676 | Elizabeth City |
| | Burgess | |

Yowell, Thomas

| | c.1644-1695 | Westmoreland |
| | Burgess | |

Z

Zouch, John

| | 1644 | Henrico |
| | Burgess | |

Black Point, Jamestown Island

Tidewater Virginia Families:
A Magazine of History and Geneaology
Volume 6, Number 3, Pg 143

CPSIA information can be obtained
at www.ICGtesting.com
Printed in the USA
FSOW04n2207060815
9621FS